CHINA

INDIA

BANGLADESH

Mekong River

Irrawaddy River

Mandalay

Shan
Plateau

MYANMAR
(BURMA)

LAOS

Red River

Hanoi

Hainan

Pagan

Taunggi

Chiang Mai

Luang
Prabang

Vientiane

*Bay of
Bengal*

Prome

*South
China
Sea*

Chao Phraya River

THAILAND

Hue

VIETNAM

Yangon
(Rangoon)

Ayutthaya

Bangkok

Angkor

*Tenasserim
Coast*

CAMBODIA

*Andaman
Sea*

Phnom Penh

Indian Ocean

*Mekong
River*

Ho Chi Minh City
(Saigon)

*Gulf of
Thailand*

Straits of Malacca

Penang

BRUNEI

MALAYSIA

MALAYSIA

Kuala Lumpur

Seremban

Malacca

Kuching

Saraw

Singapore

SINGAPORE

Padang

Kalimant

Sumatra

Jakarta

I   N

500 Km

500 Miles

Java

Ternate

Bali

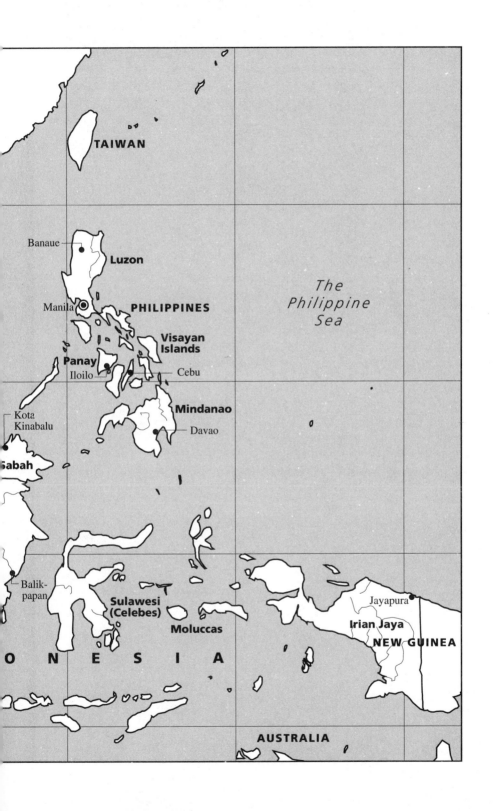

CUISINES

of

SOUTHEAST ASIA

A Culinary Journey Through
Thailand, Myanmar, Laos, Vietnam, Malaysia,
Singapore, Indonesia, and the Philippines

GWENDA L. HYMAN

John Wiley & Sons, Inc.
New York • Chichester • Brisbane • Toronto • Singapore

Publisher: Thomas Woll
Senior Editor: Claire Thompson
Managing Editor: Jacqueline A. Martin
Composition: Crane Typesetting Service, Inc.
Map of Southeast Asia: Kevin Osborne

This text is printed on acid-free paper.

This publication is designed to provide accurate and authoritative
information in regard to the subject matter covered. It is sold
with the understanding that the publisher is not engaged in
rendering professional services. If legal, accounting, medical,
psychological, or any other expert assistance is required, the
services of a competent professional person should be sought.
ADAPTED FROM A DECLARATION OF PRINCIPLES OF A JOINT COMMITTEE OF
THE AMERICAN BAR ASSOCIATION AND PUBLISHERS.

Library of Congress Cataloging-in-Publication Data:

Hyman, Gwenda L.
    Cuisines of Southeast Asia : a culinary journey through Thailand,
Myanmar, Laos, Vietnam, Malaysia, Singapore, Indonesia, and the Philippines /
Gwenda L. Hyman.
        p.   cm.
    Includes index.
    ISBN 0-471-58249-2 (alk. paper)
    1. Cookery, Southeast Asian.   2. Cookery—Southeast Asia.
I. Title.
TX724.5.S68H96   1993
641.5959—dc20
                                                                    93-1970
                                                                    CIP

Printed in the United States of America

10 9 8 7 6 5 4 3 2 1

To Chuck with love

CONTENTS

PREFACE

Although there are some excellent recipes in this book, this is not a recipe book. Rather, it is a gastronomical journey through Southeast Asia to acquaint you with cuisines that have been left largely unexplored in this country. Some of the most creative cuisines in the world are found here. You will learn how the history, geography, and religions of this region have all had an influence on this exciting food. Noodles and the wok, introduced by Chinese settlers, and the chili pepper grown in Mexico but brought to Southeast Asia by the Portuguese, have revolutionized their cooking. The basic food is rice. Very little meat is eaten, and a minimal amount of oil used. Assertive yet subtle seasonings flavor fish, poultry, and vegetable dishes, which combined with the region's luscious tropical fruits, produce some of the world's most healthful cuisines.

Southeast Asian cooking is neither difficult nor complicated. It is the simple cooking of largely rural people who are concerned with nutrition, economy, and ease of preparation. The intriguing taste lies in a blending of flavors that are clean, assertive, tart, and sweet. The basic ingredients for these flavors are lemongrass, tamarind, lime, sugar, and fish sauce. Though rudimentary, these ingredients are vital to Southeast Asian cuisine. The fresh taste evident in this food comes from an abundance of herbs, some as familiar as mint and basil, others more unusual, yet accessible to us through Asian markets. Local wild leaves, gathered daily from forest, field, and stream, add many different textures, and bursts of unexpected tangy flavor. The 2,500 species of fish flourishing in the surrounding seas provide the region's main source of protein. Twice as much fish is eaten here as anywhere else in the world. Bean curd, generally homemade, is an affordable source of protein for people living far from the sea, and a mainstay of vegetarian cuisine. Most Southeast Asians are Buddhists, and many are strictly vegetarian. A plethora of exciting meatless dishes is a unique facet of these cuisines.

Asian cuisine is in vogue right now in all the large cities of Europe and America. The number of new restaurants increases daily. Los Angeles boasts at least 200 Thai restaurants, and they also continue to proliferate in London and Paris. Asian spices and herbs are invading traditional French cuisine. Innovative chefs, eschewing butter, cream, and egg yolks, infuse their dishes with the tantalizing aromas of ginger, lemongrass, and chilies. Complex spice mixtures and lively oriental herbs, used with gusto in Southeast Asia's silken curries and fragrant stir-fries, in discreet amounts are replacing tarragon and thyme. Young American chefs on both coasts have perfumed their foods with the bright, intense flavors of the Orient for many years. French chefs, bound by the rules of a centuries-old, formal cuisine, seem to have taken a more moderate approach to these assertive spices. Now the penetrating flavors of kaffir lime, Holy basil, fish and soy sauces are adding a spark to dishes on both sides of the Atlantic. Undeniably delicious though Asian food is, part of the reason for this trend is that the cooking is light, yet satisfies the appetite and the palate while concurring with the recent guidelines for a nutritious and healthful diet.

ACKNOWLEDGMENTS

I would like to thank the many people who helped me with this book. First my husband Charles Hyman who provided a great deal of pertinent information and with unflagging zeal ate all the Southeast Asian dishes I cooked. My thanks also go to Ismail Merchant and Madhur Jaffrey, who long ago fed all of us their homemade exotic Indian dishes, and started in me a lifelong quest for new and different cuisines. My sincere thanks to Kevin Osborne who created the beautiful map of Southeast Asia for this book, and Dr. Harm de Blij of Georgetown University for his geographical expertise. For their gracious and invaluable help in lending me books from their libraries, I want to thank: Katherine Warnell, Gaye Lamb, Jacquelyn Chagnon, Development Counselor on Laos and Vietnam; Roger Rumpf of the Asia Resource Center, Bounheng Inversin, Teresita Sison and Dang Anderson. I also want to thank Mr. Vishakha N. Desai, Director of the Galleries, The Asia Society, Ms. Mirza M. Burgos of The Asia Society Galleries, Ms. Jeanne Brodsky and Ms. Eileen Sullivan of the Metropolitan Museum, the librarians at the Philippine Embassy, the Royal Thai Embassy, and the Indonesian Embassy for their assistance, and finally my editor Claire Thompson for her wise guidance and kind encouragement throughout this project.

THAILAND

Spicy, colorful Thai food, scented with an extraordinary range of herbs, roots, and seasonings, is a gastronomic delight, and possibly the most sophisticated cuisine in Southeast Asia. Thai food is always fresh. Cooked extremely quickly—the ingredients retain both their freshness and their nutrients. Meat, which plays a minor role in Thai meals, is customarily lean. Fish and shellfish, fresh daily from local waters, is less expensive than meat. Chicken is versatile and much loved whether roasted, deep-fried, curried, stir-fried, or grilled over charcoal. Meat, poultry, and seafood generally are highly seasoned with fragrant leaves, fiercely hot chilies, pungent fish sauce, and aromatic roots, such as ginger and turmeric. Influenced over the centuries by China, India, Malaysia, Indonesia, and Portugal, Thais have integrated into their cuisine with care the foreign ideas that appealed to their tastes, and the result is a seamless cuisine, uniquely their own.

Thais have intense feelings about food. Spirited discussions are held on the merits of a new restaurant, or the prowess of an old one with a new dish. The pros and cons are debated in loving detail, and with unabated enthusiasm. As it is not unusual for a city restaurant to have a minimum of 70 dishes on the menu, these considerations take time.

Thailand is very much a land of contrasts. Luxury hotels looming over squalid slums, a soaring ultramodern skyscraper proudly displaying its own ornate shrine, pungent with incense to appease the spirits; a peasant leading his water buffalo as he plows a rice paddy,

Mythical Thai lion

while a jet whines above his head; bustling markets selling simple noodle soups and imitation Patek Philippe watches. Thailand is fascinating, unique in culture, cuisine, and architecture. Its physical landscape, webbed with waterways and glittering with splendid palaces and golden temples, yields riches from rubies and sapphires to tin and rubber, and boasts the best beaches on the mainland. Thailand is one of the most highly developed nations in Southeast Asia. The country is shaped rather like the profile of an elephant head. The forehead abuts Myanmar, the outer edge of the wide ear borders Laos to the east, the trunk forms the long Malay peninsula, and the mouth is Bangkok, Thailand's capital city. At one time their flag depicted a red elephant on a white ground. The King changed it to three wide stripes of red, white, and blue after Thailand joined the League of Nations. Thailand is the heart of mainland Southeast Asia. Neighboring Myanmar to the northwest and Thailand share the upper strip of the Malay Peninsula. The central strip is Thai territory, and the lower Malaysian. The eastern coastline of the 600-mile-long peninsula is lapped by the waters of the Gulf of Thailand. Cambodia sits directly across the Gulf, and the southernmost tip of Vietnam's long coastline curves beneath Cambodia. Landlocked Laos stretches from the Myanmar border in the north to the Cambodian border in the south, along Thailand's northeastern region.

Most of the hilltribe people, originally from China, live in mountainous areas. Many of them hold animistic beliefs. Six main hilltribes
live in the northern region, each with their own language, culture, and
history. The six main groups are Akha, Hmong, Karen, Lahn, Lisu,
and Mien. The Christian Karen, descended from Tibeto-Burmans, are
matrilineal. Karens only marry within their own tribe. Some own
elephants and work in the teak forests as mahouts. The Akha tribe
originated from Yunnan Province in China. Their villages, guarded by
sacred gates erected to keep evil spirits at bay, are easily identified
by the heavy thatching on the roofs of the houses. Akha women wear
spectacular red and black tribal dress and a heavy helmet-shaped
close-fitting headdress, every inch of which is decorated with silver
coins, beads, and long ornaments. These women are well known
for their weaving expertise. Some of the massive turbans worn by
tribeswomen have silver ornaments suspended from the front, and
brightly colored pom-poms piled on top. Silver ornaments brighten
tunic hems, jacket edges, and the legs of baggy pants.

The hill people are very poor. Because their land is not suitable
for wet rice growing, they practice the destructive slash-and-burn
technique. At one time opium was the main cash crop grown in the
Golden Triangle formed by the intersection of Thailand, Myanmar,
and Laos. Recently, tea and tobacco planting is replacing opium.

Chiang Mai, one of the oldest towns in Northern Thailand, has
become a thriving tourist attraction. Known as the Rose of the North,
Chiang Mai is Bangkok's favorite escape from the heat. Situated in
dense teak-forested mountains, this ancient city is filled with flowers
in the winter months. Apples, grapes, strawberries, and dozens of
different vegetables, which would perish in the steamy heat of the
lowlands, bloom and thrive in its cool climate. Tourists flock to Chiang
Mai in February every year for its huge Flower Festival. Northern
people are strongly influenced by neighboring Myanmar in their art,
their architecture, and their food. They follow the Myanmar people's
fondness for pork. The best pork butchers in the kingdom are in
Chiang Mai and charcuterie is their specialty. Ban Yon, the wife of
one of these famed butchers, is known all over Thailand for her
sausage, called *nam*. Made from a mixture of raw ground pork, ground
pork rind, and heavily laced with salt, garlic, and chilies, *nam* is molded
in a clay pot and left to mature for three days. Only then does it reach

its peak of perfection. The salt, garlic, and chilies preserve the raw sausage meat. Some devotées insist on waiting five days before digging into Ban Yon's famous dish. With increasing demand, and more modern methods of packaging, *nam* is no longer encased in clay, but is rolled first in cellophane, and then in a banana leaf.

Northern cuisine is heavier than southern. Oil is used in larger quantities. Sticky or glutinous rice is preferred to long-grain dry rice. It is easy to knead glutinous rice into balls to sop up the sauces and push food around the plate. Ripe mangoes, sliced over sticky rice and topped with rich sweet coconut cream, is a traditional Chiang Mai dessert. Fried noodles are another favorite. *Kow Soy*, a popular coconut milk curry, is accompanied by crispy noodles for dunking. Pickled cucumber is served with dishes of fried pork crackling, boiled cabbage, egg noodles, and also with all pork curries. Minced pork is an ingredient in a number of dishes. *Nam Prik Ong* mixes minced pork with tomatoes, chilies, garlic, and shrimp paste. Chilled, it is served with pork rind, cabbage, and cucumbers.

The northeastern area of Thailand has a wealth of ancient monuments, many of them built by the Khmers, who colonized the northeastern part of Thailand while they were building Angkor Wat in the twelfth century. Some of the dialects spoken in this region, and much of the cuisine, is more similar to those of Laos and Cambodia than to that of Thailand. One major site at Phimai, restored by the Thai government, has been dubbed the "Angkor Wat of Thailand." It is fast becoming a major tourist attraction.

Northeastern cuisine also favors minced pork. One famous dish, called *larb*, made with either minced pork, beef, chicken, or fish, is eaten raw accompanied by a searing hot condiment. This is followed by mint leaves to cool the palate. Closely resembling the cooking of Laos to the east, dried beef, grilled chicken, and an abundant use of herbs and hot chilies distinguish this region's cuisine. Green papaya salad seasoned with lime, chilies, and dried shrimp is a favorite throughout Southeast Asia.

A major archaeological site, near the small northeastern village of Ban Chiang, has proven the existence of a prehistoric culture more than 5,000 years old. The people who lived there were adept not only at weaving, rice cultivation, and animal husbandry, but also made tools and ornaments from bronze. Intricately designed and painted pottery, unearthed at a road building site, initiated the dig. Thailand has now replaced China and Mesopotamia as the nation with the first bronze-using society in the world.

Religious statues indicate that Hindu people inhabited what is now southern Thailand in the fourth century A.D. In the ninth century, people from southern and central China, possibly fleeing the Mongol invasions, sought refuge in Thailand. Their first major city, Sukhothai, or "Dawn of Happiness," was built in the middle of the Central Plain. Thai written language, culture, architecture, and their Buddhist religion were well established when repeated attacks from marauders forced the Thais to flee farther south. In 1351, they founded the city of Ayutthaya. A splendid metropolis of lavish palaces and soaring temples with gold statues of the Buddha, Ayutthaya ruled over all the terrain that is now Thailand, and also parts of Burma, China, Laos, Cambodia, and Malaysia for 400 years. In the early 1500s, European emissaries from Portugal, Holland, and Britain came to Thailand and on their return to Europe they told wondrous tales of the fabulous city of the east. Inevitably calamity fell. In 1767, Burmese hoards, burning and looting, overran Ayutthaya, reduced the population of 1 million to 10,000, and left the city in ruins. Gathering together scholars and storytellers to restore the Siamese heritage, the first Chakri king in the present ruling Chakri Dynasty built another city on the shores of the Gulf of Thailand, near present-day Bangkok. He also extended the borders to include the northern mountains and the long southern neck of land between the Gulf and the Andaman Sea.

Succeeding monarchs, particularly King Mongkut (1851–1868) of Anna and "The King and I" fame, and his son King Chulalongkorn (1868–1910), steered the state toward modernization, and established the country's infrastructure. King Chulalongkorn launched the vast canal-building project that today criss-crosses the fertile Central Plain, providing water for a sea of gently waving, emerald green rice shoots. By skillful diplomacy, and by relinquishing parts of the kingdom, Thailand evaded colonization by the French. As recently as the mid-1940s, Thailand was the only independent country on the mainland: Laos, Cambodia, and Vietnam were French colonies and Malaysia, Burma, and the Indian continent were British. It was in 1932 that the name of the country was changed from Siam to Thailand, meaning "the Land of the Free." At the same time, and without bloodshed, the absolute rule of the king was changed to a constitutional monarchy.

The spectacular bicentennial celebration of the reigning Chakri dynasty was held in October 1982. All monarchs bear the name "Rama" after their own names and titles. King Bhumibol Adulyadej, Rama IX, and his beautiful wife, Queen Sirikit, though immensely popular, are regarded with awe and reverence. At court, people approach the King on their knees. Protocol dictates that no one be allowed to have his head higher than that of His Majesty. When the Royal cars appear on Bangkok's streets, construction workers slide down their bamboo scaffolding with dispatch to avoid having their heads higher than the King's!

The King and Queen have earned the people's high regard. King Bhumibol has been untiring in his efforts to better the lives of his 55 million subjects. He has introduced scores of new crops, especially to the Golden Triangle area where he hopes to replace opium growing. At King Bhumibol's urging, the government provides seeds, fertilizers, and other technical assistance to the farmers. The 3 square miles (4.5 square kilometers) of grounds around the royal residence, Chitralada Palace, in Bangkok, are used for experimental farming. King Bhumibol travels tirelessly around his kingdom, talking to his subjects and offering solutions to their problems. Queen Sirikit travels with him, working to improve the lot of the impoverished hilltribes people by having them instructed in craft making, to increase their income. A project of Queen Sirikit's is the development of silkworm nurseries. The increased silk yield goes to the making of export-quality silk fabrics, hand woven by the hilltribes.

Rice—the Wealth of the Kingdom

Each year the King presides over an ancient, solemn rice ceremony as plowing time draws near, on the Pramane Ground outside the walls of the Grand Palace. The ceremony begins with the priests offering special delicacies to the Gods. Then two oxen, splendidly draped with cloth of gold, pulling the ceremonial plough, are led before the King. Women scatter rice from silver and gold ceremonial dishes, and Brahmins sprinkle holy water. The oxen are presented with grains, beans, and alcohol. Their choice symbolizes the success or failure of the year's rice crop. Alcohol would not augur well.

For 700 years, rice, the wealth of the kingdom, has fed the people of Thailand. Every Thai is acutely aware that the rice farmer is the backbone of the nation. Children are taught never to sweep up spilled rice with a broom, but to bend their backs to pick up each precious grain as homage to the rice farmer who labors so hard to feed them. Rice is vital to the people of the kingdom, and, as their principal export crop, to the economy of Thailand. The heart of Thailand, and where most of the people live, is the milewide Central Plain. Extremely fertile alluvial soils, deposited by the Chao Phraya River which bisects the Plain, form this vast rice bowl. Water buffalo still plow the rice paddies at the end of the dry season, though mechanized plows, called iron buffaloes, are in use in some areas. In May when the monsoon rains come, the whole community works to plant the fragile shoots. Men and women, wearing large straw hats shaped rather like lamp shades, may be seen bending double, calf-deep in the gleaming water. Scallions are planted along the edges of the rice paddies.

When the rains come and flood the fields, young taliapin, a delicate white-fleshed fish, are slipped into the flooded paddies to mature alongside the rice. The floodwaters bring nutrients from the highland forest floors which nourish the rice. Irrigation systems or well-maintained dikes control the water at exactly the right level for the lengthening shoots. Being able to control the water of major rivers and their tributaries enables the farmers to grow more than one crop a year. If the river system flows year round, then the farmers, working together on digging, plowing, and planting, can produce three or more crops. After the harvest in November, huge woven baskets are used to winnow the ripened grain. Surplus rice is taken down the narrow waterways to waiting barges on the Chao Phraya River. Resuming its journey, the rice is later transferred to cargo ships, to be exported from the port of Bangkok.

Wooden farmhouses, some low and roofed in bamboo matting, others elegantly built on stilts, cluster along the banks of the waterways. Each dwelling houses the entire extended family with room for the water buffalo. The day starts early for farming families, usually before dawn. The first meal of the day is cooked in a wok, over a charcoal stove placed on the little jetty beside the *klong* (waterway).

Fishing nets, with umbrella-like spokes, hang from the jetty to catch any unwary fish. Beside the house a small garden plot grows vegetables, herbs, and usually a banana plant. Inside the house a small shrine holds an offering of fruit or flowers. Above the housetops may be glimpsed the glittering red and gold spire of a temple. They seem to be floating on an emerald green sea. Farmers produce not only rice but fruits, vegetables, betel nut, poultry, and livestock. Usually the women in the family, their boats loaded with produce, spices, pickled garlic, curry pastes, and dewy fresh noodles, make the journey by water to the markets in Bangkok.

Bangkok—known as Krung Thep, or City of Angels to the Thais—was modeled originally on Ayutthaya, the ancient city whose thoroughfares were not roads but canals, encircling the city. The canals acted as moats, affording protection in time of need. Rivers and canals were Thailand's thoroughfares for centuries. Eventually Bangkok's circular canals were connected by smaller canals to form a vast web of waterways. Man-made and natural waterways, within and between villages, are still the main means of travel today. Many villagers use their boats to commute. Small round sampans and the long-tailed slender motorboats skim the surface of the water. Possibly originating in Thailand, the propeller and motor are designed for use in shallow water. They are indispensable in both *klongs* and rice paddies. Building roads that would only flood during the monsoon rains seemed imprudent. Even so, the new roads have made it much easier for people in once remote villages to bring goods to market. In Bangkok, canals that have been paved over to accommodate the increasing four-wheeled transportation overflow during the monsoon rains, inundating whole neighborhoods. Bangkok today is a thriving, up-to-date city, sprawled over an area of 930 square miles (1,500 square kilometers), and rapidly changing as it adapts to the latest in modern technology, and to the unending influx of foreign ideas. Traffic is an enormous problem in Bangkok. Cars, buses, and small trucks overflowing with produce clog streets, creating pollution and gridlock. Motorcycles, decorated with a kaleidoscope of gaudy designs, are everywhere. Motorized taxis, called tuk tuks, have replaced the pedicabs. Vendors dart fearlessly into the stalled traffic, hawking garlands of jasmine blossoms for placing at shrines or revitalizing snacks for the frustrated motorists.

The architecture of Bangkok is eclectic: contemporary office blocks, such as Baiyoke Tower at Pratunam, tower 490 feet (150 meters) over tiny family-owned shop-houses, their living quarters on the second floor, which at one time made up the greater part of the structures lining the city streets. The new architecture exists happily alongside the gorgeously decorative, classical architecture of palaces, state buildings, and numerous *wats* or temples built by earlier generations. Gilded ornaments embellish multiple-tiered roofs of dark green and red tiles. Golden *chedi*, or spires, glitter in the sunlight. Fierce lions and guardian warriors of gold guard the outside of the temples, while within gilded statues of Buddha, wreathed in incense, sit before flickering candles and heaps of flowers.

An extraordinary legend surrounds a solid gold Buddha weighing five and a half tons, with sapphire and mother-of-pearl eyes which sits in *wat* Traimitr in Bangkok. Apparently this huge, gold Buddha was plastered over by a monk to conceal its worth from invading Burmese hoards in Ayutthaya. Enshrined in a temple on the riverbank, it was discovered in 1950 by a construction company, when the enormous statue had to be moved. The chain from which the statue was suspended broke, and the fall cracked the plaster coating, revealing the gleaming gold Buddha.

Wat *Phra Keo* houses the Emerald Buddha—the most revered Buddha image in Thailand. It was discovered in 1434 in the city of Chiang Rai. For centuries the Emerald Buddha was moved from temple to temple, both in Laos and Thailand, finally coming to rest, at the behest of Rama I, in the Royal Chapel in the Grand Palace enclosure, where it is on display.

Thais love color with a passion. Huge, hand-painted advertising billboards promoting shows, movies, discos, and commercial products embellish the sides of buildings. They are painted a section at a time by teams of artists, watched from below by enthusiastic crowds. Discos are big business. The stage sets created for well-loved pop singers are often incredibly imaginative, with gorgeous costumes, laser lighting, and blaring music. Bangkok is crowded and nowhere more so than the famous Weekend Market. Canvas-covered stalls sell quantities of foodstuffs, and also herbal medicines, caged songbirds, and tropical fish. The Floating Market outside Bangkok, called Damnern Saduak, is even more popular, especially with camera-toting tourists. The waterborne vendors, dressed in baggy pants, long blue shirts, and straw hats, sell luscious, freshly picked fruits and vegetables from their sampans. Gridlock results when the vendors, competing for customers, try to shove their boats in the same direction all at the same time. At the edge of the *klong* women cook nutritious snacks with lightning speed for waiting patrons.

Foodstalls lining the Bangkok streets offer a wide selection of tempting snacks, fruits, and prepared dishes, from delicate savory meatballs to fiery curries. Attempts to tidy up the streets by moving the foodstalls to market areas have been unsuccessful. Thais are inveterate snackers. Street vendors are a traditional part of Bangkok life. They are well patronized by housewives, busy office workers at lunch time, or anyone else who wants either to eat on the spot or to buy time-saving, ready-made items to take home. Not surprisingly, foodstalls teem around markets, selling the freshest of fresh food, displayed in ways that are pleasing to the eye and tempting to the palate. Pyramids of freshly made quenelles, twists of fresh noodles in myriad sizes and shapes, tiers of tiny meatballs, carefully made from beef or pork in the wee hours of the morning before being brought to market, stacks of mouthwatering fruits and crunchy vegetables, lovingly arranged into neat patterns, greet the eye at every turn. Street vendors move from place to place with their wares, often pushing a bicycle fitted with a parasol for coolness and a large case to display the tempting wares. Others set up stalls wherever they are able to find a spot—perhaps beside a cool *klong* or outside a store—and sell delicious treats made from rice, cooked in a bamboo tube or folded in a piece of banana leaf; mango with rice and coconut cream or unbelievably juicy, sweet pineapple. If a vendor's specialty needs to be cooked on the spot, *satays*, for example, the vendor will even carry a charcoal stove. Noodle sellers also carry stoves for frying or simmering fresh noodles in spicy broth. Most noodle shops stay open all night in Bangkok, catering to the people who frequent the swinging nightclubs, bars, and discos. Thais love to party all night, and the bright lights of the noodle shops, glowing in the dark, provide a welcome to hungry revelers who need a little sustenance before the journey home.

Charcoal-burning stove

Buddhism in The Land of Smiles

The people of Thailand, often called "The Land of Smiles," are known for their gentle dispositions, their open-handed hospitality, and their perfect politeness—no matter how trying the circumstances. The Buddhist philosophy which guides all aspects of their day-to-day existence brings tranquility, and a joyful acceptance of their lot. Thais have an irrepressible sense of humor—called *sanuk*—which turns whatever they are doing into fun. *Sanuk* is the essence of their lives and they find it in work or play, and also in their frequent religious ceremonies. Thailand is unique in that it does not have the multiplicity of religions and language that divide people in some parts of Southeast Asia. Almost 90 percent of the people speak Thai and 95 percent are Buddhists. Thais are Buddhists of the Theravada orthodoxy—the teaching closest to that of the Buddha. The Myanmar, Lao, and Cambodians also adhere to this faith. Buddhism, headed by the Supreme Patriarch, plays a pivotal role in the behavior and social interaction of the Thai people, and has done so for centuries. Religion permeates their lives, and 27,000 glittering fanciful *wats* attest to the prevalence of the Buddhist faith.

Thais believe that performing religious duties on earth is the way to ensure advancement in future reincarnations. Great importance is attached to earning merit. Each year journeys to remote villages are undertaken joyfully to bring new saffron robes to the monks, or to help build or repair temples. Buddhists think that the soul is held prisoner within the body until death liberates it. Cremation, in a boat-shaped pyre to speed the soul on its journey, is an occasion for joy. Despite the Thais' unswerving faith in Buddhism, they are surprisingly tolerant of other religions. Indonesia and Malaysia are 90 percent Muslim. Indian missionaries brought the Hindu religion to the archipelagos, and, to this day, the Balinese are fervent happy Hindus. The Philippines owe their Roman Catholicism to their Spanish conquerors. Pockets of all these religions exist in Thailand, along with strongly held animistic beliefs. Nevertheless, Buddhism reigns supreme. The focus of each Buddhist community is the *wat*, where all festivals, village meetings, and community events are held. Monks are called upon for advice and to arbitrate disputes. Within the temple complex, children attend government schools taught by the brotherhood.

For the three months of the wet season, it is customary for young men to enter a monastery. Some stay longer, of course, and some stay for life. Most men in Thailand, including King Bhumibol, have participated for a short time in the monastic life. Thais feel a man is not "seasoned" until he has done so, and few women would want to marry a man who had not fulfilled this obligation. In rural areas, entering the monastery is a cause for huge celebration. The day before the ceremony, delicious cooking smells waft over the village. Great vats of rice are boiled, and whole suckling pigs and sides of meat are roasted to crisp brown succulence. On the great day, the heads of the novitiates are shaven, and they are clothed in fine white garments fringed with gold. Carried shoulder-high in procession to the temple, they will spend their time purifying their bodies and souls through prayer and abstinence. Wearing the saffron robes of the brotherhood, in the early morning they will beg for their daily meal. Monks eat only between sunrise and noon.

Buddhism and strong animist beliefs are interwoven in Thailand. When a Thai family builds a house they establish themselves in their new dwelling not just physically but also spiritually. Most Thais believe that the ground they build on, the wood they build with, and also the surrounding hills, rivers, and forests have a spirit dwelling within them. These spirits have to be propitiated, or even enlisted to help the family, by means of offerings and incantations. In some cases a spirit may need to be exorcised. These animist beliefs coexist quite happily with Buddhism. Before the building of the house can begin, an auspicious date is chosen by an astrologer or by a monk. The floor of the dwelling is raised well above ground level, not only to prevent flooding or insect invasion, but to lift the inhabitants of the house above possibly hostile spirits. These beliefs are universal in Thailand. In the city the ceremony for opening a modern computer-filled office block would have a ceremony at the same time for the opening of the elaborate and costly spirit house for the dispossessed spirits of the ground the new business is built upon. The time and date selected for the ceremony involves a great deal of complicated astrological consultation. Offerings of food, flowers, and incense are placed regularly before the spirit house to ensure the success of the enterprise. Spirit houses are also seen in forests and by rivers, where many offerings are made for the success of the rice harvest.

In the rural south, rice is still the basis of the economy, though the rubber plantations, introduced by the British, still thrive. Thailand's healthy international balance of payments is sustained by many agricultural products, such as rice, corn, beans, sugar, tobacco, coconuts, soy beans, pineapples, and cassava—from which tapioca flour is made. Tin, rubies, and sapphires are all mined for export. Japan taught the Thais how to seed their oyster beds in the southern waters off the peninsula, and how to harvest pearls. Oil and natural gas fields in the Gulf contribute to the economy. And now the tourist trade is burgeoning, attracted by crystal clear water, and mile upon mile of pristine beaches. Of interest to tourists is the network of new roads, built with the help of America's military during the Vietnam War, which have made it easier to reach the archeological monuments in the north and the beaches in the south.

Southern Thai cuisine is synonymous with northern Malaysian cuisine. Throughout its long history, the narrow stretch of land separating the Andaman Sea and the Gulf of Thailand has alternated between Thai dominion and Malaysian dominion. Numerous southern recipes follow Islamic food taboos, and not surprisingly, these heavily spiced, rice-based dishes, augmented with chicken, dried shrimp, or fermented fish, are claimed as national fare by both countries. *Knanom Chin*, a common southern breakfast dish, is made with rice noodles and shredded beef spiced with chili and paprika. Beloved for its keeping qualities by travelers, especially seamen, is a curry that has simmered for a full seven days. The majority of southern dishes feature the fresh catch from the rich fishing grounds on both sides of the peninsula.

The Cuisine of Thailand

Precise proportions and explicit rules for seasonings set Thai food apart from the somewhat hit-and-miss approach used in some Southeast Asian countries. Premixed curry pastes, sausages, meatballs, fish quenelles, and ready-made fresh noodles may be relied on to give predictable results. Possibly because of the arduous work involved in grinding spices and chopping ingredients by hand, prepared items are widely used. Curry pastes constantly in demand are an extremely hot orange-colored mixture, made from the hottest pepper in the world—*phrik khi nu luang*; a light green fiery paste from the "bird" chili—*phrik khi nu*; a red paste made from dried red chilies and paprika; and a yellow, spice-laden paste redolent of turmeric. Mounds of these spicy mixtures are freshly made each day, and sold in markets and shops all over Thailand. Asian markets in major American cities also carry these curry pastes.

The heat comes from capsaicin stored in the ribs of the chili peppers which spreads to the seeds when the chilies are handled. Tasting a piece cut from the pepper, without ribs or seeds, helps decide which dishes they will complement. Capsaicin will burn whatever it touches and is both painful and long lasting, so wearing rubber gloves when handling chilies, and washing hands, utensils, and all surfaces with hot, soapy water afterward is a good idea.

Chilies belong to the genus Capsicum. A confusing number of similar-looking varieties of chili pepper exist, though the tastes may differ greatly. Chilies cross-pollinate with abandon, adding to the confusion, and it is virtually impossible to know without tasting a sliver how hot they are. Chilies that look the same as the Cayenne chili available here in Asian markets pack a wallop. The fleshy, conical-

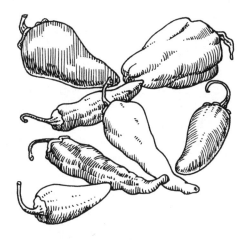

Chilies

shaped, green variety, which corresponds to the Jalapeno so popular in the United States, is medium hot. Several dried varieties are used to make chili oil, hot bean sauces, and chili and garlic sauce. Dried chilies may be lightly toasted to enhance their flavor before adding them to the dish, where they will reconstitute in the sauce. Or they may be soaked for 30 minutes to facilitate slicing or mincing. Roasting unripe, green chilies will eliminate any bitterness present in the skin. Red chilies have already ripened and taste sweeter. Generally the larger fleshier peppers, look-alikes for our Banana and Poblano peppers, are sliced into curries and stir-fries. All chili peppers, whether hot or not, give color and an intense herbal taste to corn, curries, chicken, baked fish, grilled steaks, stir-fries, rice, and other grain dishes.

The Portuguese introduced chilies to Southeast Asia, India, and Africa in the fifteenth century, where they have had a profound influence on the cuisines. Any Southeast Asian recipe that gets its spicy heat from peppercorns predates the arrival of the Portuguese traders.

In Thailand, a small bowl of *nam prik phao*, containing red chilies, roasted scallions, roasted garlic, lime juice, and fish sauce is always at hand as a dipping sauce and as a condiment for everybody to mix with their own food, and thus select their preferred ratio of Btus. All cooks have their own version of *nam prik phao*, so innumerable recipes exist for this blazing sauce.

For most Thais, breakfast consists of a soft, soupy rice porridge, called *khao tom*, made by cooking rice with twice the normal amount of water. Served with flakes of fish or salted fish, meat, or pickles, it is sometimes topped with an egg. Lunch is invariably noodles. These are all prevailing, so much so that frequently, office workers will begin their meal with soupy noodles garnished with fish or meatballs, and end with a helping of crispy fried noodles. Two favorites at lunchtime are *Pad Thai* and *Mee Krob*. *Pad Thai* is highly seasoned noodles with vegetables and tofu. *Mee Krob* is fried noodles topped with a caramelized ground meat sauce. The crunchy texture and sweet sauce of this dish add balance to a menu featuring satiny coconut curries. In the nineteenth century, King Chulalongkorn decreed that Thais should give up eating with chopsticks and instead use spoons and forks. They complied, except when it came to noodles, which are still eaten with chopsticks.

A Thai evening meal might consist of a creamy, mild chicken soup with lemon and cilantro; a fried noodle dish, a fresh vegetable salad, a fiery beef curry laced with red chilies; a crisp, fried fish with a hot condiment; a stir-fry of crunchy water chestnuts, ginger, and shrimp; and perhaps an omelette stuffed with well-flavored ground pork. Salads and other vegetables play a large part in Thai meals. One famous hearty salad, called *Yam Yai*, is a national favorite. Well-planned meals would have a balance of hot, mild, sour, sweet, and bitter dishes and smooth, crisp, creamy, and crunchy textures. Vegetables, neatly sliced and cooked for only a few seconds, retain their distinctive shapes and bright colors. Several small entrées are served together at each meal, including bowls of steaming soup. Soup is an integral part of a Thai meal. Served daily, it is often flavored with lemongrass and cilantro. The main emphasis is on the huge mound of hot, fluffy, white rice. Everyone helps themselves to rice first and then a little of whatever appeals to them, mixing the savory morsels with the rice. This way a

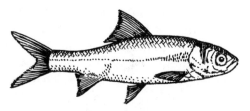

Pla nuan chan (carp)

Cilantro

particularly scorching chili-laced food may be followed by a soothing mouthful of a milder dish—perhaps a creamy coconut soup, or a forkful of fresh green leaves. People often say that Thai food has three flavors—hot, hotter, and hottest. There is some truth to this, but it is by no means the whole truth. Mild and subtle dishes are just as prevalent as scorching ones laden with chilies.

Desserts are reserved for special occasions. A healthy substitute is a generous helping of the wonderful fresh fruit for which Thailand is famous. Served peeled, sliced, and pleasingly arranged, fruit is a soothing finish after a spicy meal. Always available are papaya, pineapple, watermelon, and many varieties of bananas. Seasonal fruits served frequently are pomelos, rambutan, jackfruit, and mangosteen. Durian, a spiky green fruit, the size of a rugby ball, has creamy flesh and a luscious taste that is ambrosial. Lovers of durian are rapturous in their praise, but be warned, the descriptions of the smell upon cutting open the durian are for the most part unprintable: rotten cheese is the politest. Feast days warrant desserts. Customarily two are presented—one "liquid" and one "dry." The liquid desserts comprise fruits in syrup or coconut cream; a baked mung bean custard made with eggs, sugar, and coconut milk; lotus seeds in coconut milk; or the famous dessert from Chiang Mai—sliced mango with sticky rice. "Dry" desserts may be candies, crystallized fruits, small cakes of sweetened fruit pastes, or stiffened fruit gelatin squares. Thais are extremely fond of candy and consume great quantities. Candy making in Thailand is an art, but the recipes are often too complex or time-consuming to make at home. South of Bangkok, at Petchaburi, is a well-known candy factory, restaurant, and market combined. Superb confections, freshly made from lotus seeds, coconut cream, tapioca, vermicelli, and fruits, make the journey to Petchaburi to visit this emporium very worthwhile.

Sometimes Thais drink greatly diluted whiskey during dinner, and before the evening meal with snacks, such as nuts, bits of spicy sausage, or cubes of raw vegetables. The preferred beer is Singha and the preference in spirits is Mekong whiskey that is distilled from rice. Iced coffee has replaced Chinese tea in popularity. Delicious iced fruit juices are consumed during the day—usually purchased at sidewalk foodstalls.

How the food is presented is very important in Thailand. Thais are famous for their skillfully carved fruits and vegetables. Simple decorations, such as a red chili thinly sliced to look like a flower, or a piece of fruit carved to resemble a fan, will suffice for everyday meals. But for special occasions—a wedding, a formal reception, or the opening of a new hotel or restaurant—the services of a professional carver are engaged. The artistry involved in sectioning, cutting, and bending fruits, until the finished creation looks like an airy bouquet of real flowers blooming on the plate, is considerable. Great pride is taken in the appeal to the eye as well as the palate. Thais feel food preparation is a labor of love, and an offering to family and friends. Food even earns merit when placed in a monk's begging bowl, at a shrine, or before a statue of the Buddha. Both food and religion play a part in most significant occasions. A monk, present at the blessing of a new house, will be offered choice foods. Only the best and most rarified of dishes are served at a wedding ceremony and also at the feast which celebrates a young man's entry into a monastery. Cooking goes on for days before a wedding, and feasting continues for just as long after the event.

However, a Cordon Bleu cooking course is not necessary to grasp the fundamentals of Thai cooking. This exciting cuisine is essentially simple, quick, and easy. Fresh fish, meat, chicken, and vegetables are all neatly sliced into small pieces ahead of time, and the actual cooking usually takes ten minutes or less. A long-handled wok is placed over high heat, and the sliced foods are not so much stir-fried as briskly turned to sear all surfaces for just a few seconds in a tablespoon or two of hot oil. Retaining the food's bright color, texture, and flavor is essential.

Thai kitchens are equipped with a wok, a mortar and pestle, a grinding stone, a chopping block, and an electric rice steamer, usually the only electric utensil most Thai cooks use. A heavy-bottomed, lidded pan and a very low flame are a good substitute. There is no substitute, however, for really sharp knives for finely slicing meats and vegetables. Thai cooking is rapid. When slicing ingredients ahead of time, think small. Another practical utensil is a sizeable steamer for fish, meat, poultry, dumplings, and vegetables. The steaming time is calculated from the second the water comes to a rolling boil. Grilling is also popular, generally outdoors over an open charcoal fire with a metal grate.

The distinctive tastes of chili, cilantro, and lemongrass are easy to identify. As you would expect, with the Spice Islands on Thailand's doorstep, many more spices and seasonings perfume authentic Thai food. These include bay, mace, cumin, cloves, garlic, nutmeg, cardamom, cinnamon, peppercorns, chili powder, star anise, sesame seeds, and coriander seeds.

Recipes from Thailand

Green Curry Beef

3 T.	peanut oil
1 clove	garlic, minced
2 small	Japanese eggplants, sliced ½-inch thick
¼ lb.	quartered mushrooms
1–2 T.	Green Curry paste*

---

*obtainable in Asian markets

½ C.	coconut milk
2 T.	fish sauce
½ t.	sugar
10 oz.	lean beef, thinly sliced
½ C.	broth
3	Kaffir lime leaves, slivered
16	Holy basil leaves
	lime wedges

Heat wok, swirl oil around inside wok, add garlic, and stir-fry until lightly browned. Add eggplants and mushrooms and stir-fry until almost tender. Stir in curry paste, mixing well. Slowly add coconut milk and cook for a few minutes. Add the fish sauce, sugar, and beef, stirring until the meat is no longer pink. Stir in broth and lime leaves and simmer for 2–3 minutes. Remove from heat. Stir in basil leaves and serve immediately. Pass lime wedges separately.   *Serves 4*

Coconut Ginger Chicken Soup

	half of a chicken breast
2½ C.	chicken broth
2 strips	lemon zest
	1-inch piece of fresh ginger, sliced
3 T.	fish sauce
	2-inch inner stalk lemongrass, minced
1 C.	coconut milk
1 can	straw mushrooms
	fresh coriander leaves for garnish

Slice chicken into small cubes, and set aside. In a large saucepan over medium heat, bring to the boil the chicken broth, citrus zest, ginger, and fish sauce. Reduce heat and simmer for 3 minutes. Strain soup and return to pan, discarding solids. Return to simmer, add lemongrass, chicken, and coconut milk. Cook for 2–3 minutes or until chicken is opaque. Stir in straw mushrooms and bring to the boil. Immediately remove from heat and serve in shallow bowls, garnished with whole coriander leaves.   *Serves 6*

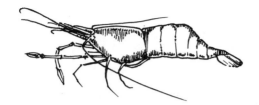

Shrimp Satay with Peanut Sauce

2	lb.	fresh shrimp
1½	T.	prepared Red Curry paste*
½	t.	salt
1	T.	sugar
1	C.	coconut milk
1	T.	rice vinegar
		canned pickled cucumber*
		Peanut Sauce mix*
		bamboo skewers, soaked in water for two hours

Shell and devein shrimp. Mix the Red Curry paste, salt, and sugar and stir in the shrimp. Marinate 5 minutes. Pour over ½ C. coconut milk and mix thoroughly. Stir in the vinegar and marinate for 1 hour. Thread the shrimp on bamboo skewers and broil for 4 or 5 minutes or until cooked through, turning the skewer over halfway through the cooking time and brushing with additional coconut milk. Serve at once with pickled cucumber and peanut sauce.   *Serves 6*

Chicken with Bamboo Shoots in Red Curry Sauce

1½	lb.	boneless chicken breast
2	T.	peanut oil
2	cloves	garlic, chopped
1½	T.	Red Curry paste*
2	T.	fish sauce
2	C.	coconut milk
⅔	C.	chicken broth

---

*obtainable in Asian markets

½ t.	sugar
	2-inch inner stalk lemongrass, slivered
1 can	whole bamboo shoots, thinly sliced
6–8	fresh basil leaves, cut in strips

Thinly slice chicken breasts and set aside. In a wok or a large skillet, heat oil and stir-fry garlic for 1 minute. Stir in curry paste and seasoning sauce and cook for 1 minute. Add chicken, pour over coconut milk, stock, sugar, and lemongrass and cook, stirring well, for 2–3 minutes or until chicken is cooked. Add bamboo shoots and basil. Bring to the simmer and stir-fry for 1 minute more.   *Serves 6*

Pork-filled Egg Sheet

1½ T.	light soy sauce
2 T.	fish sauce
1½ T.	tomato sauce
½ t.	freshly ground white pepper
2	garlic cloves
1	shallot
2	fresh water chestnuts
2	tender asparagus spears
¼ small	red bell pepper
2	plum tomatoes, seeded and chopped
1 T.	peanut oil
4 oz.	ground pork
1 t.	cumin seeds, freshly ground
4 large	eggs
2 T.	water
	fresh ground white pepper and salt, to taste
1 t.	peanut oil

In a small bowl mix together soy sauce, fish sauce, tomato sauce, and white pepper. Set aside. In a food processor mince garlic, shallot, water chestnuts, asparagus, and bell pepper. Over high heat using a wok or large skillet, heat peanut oil and stir-fry the ground pork and cumin briefly; then add the chopped vegetables and continue to stir-fry for 3 minutes longer. Set aside. Beat the eggs, water, salt, and pepper in a small bowl. In a large skillet, heat one teaspoon of oil over high heat, pour in the eggs, and tilting the pan back and forth, coat the entire surface of the pan with a thin film of egg mixture. Cook until just set. Spread pork filling in center of egg sheet, turn over sides to cover and form a squarish packet. Slide onto a platter and keep warm. To serve, slice into strips. *Serves 6*

Spinach and Fresh Shiitake Mushrooms in Sake

4 bags	spinach—2–3 lb.
4 oz.	shiitake mushrooms
1 T.	peanut oil
2	garlic cloves, thinly sliced
	pinch of salt
⅓ C.	sake rice wine

Preheat oven to 325°F. Wash spinach and discard tough stems. Spin dry. Remove stems from mushrooms and discard. Wipe mushrooms thoroughly with a damp cloth. In a saucepan large enough to hold all the spinach, heat peanut oil over medium low heat, briefly stir in garlic slices, add spinach stirring to coat. Cover and steam briefly to wilt spinach. Transfer spinach to a lidded medium-sized heatproof dish. Arrange shiitake over spinach, and sprinkle with sake. Cover and cook for 45 minutes. Serve hot. *Serves 2–3*

Thai Chicken Salad

Dressing

3 T.	fresh lime juice
2 T.	rice wine vinegar
3 T.	fish sauce
	pinch of sugar
1 clove	garlic, crushed
1 slice	fresh ginger, very finely minced
½ C.	peanut oil

Combine all ingredients, beat well, and set aside.

Rice noodle garnish

	peanut oil for frying
2 oz.	rice stick noodles

Heat oil in wok (the oil should be about an inch deep) and drop in rice sticks a few at a time. They will immediately puff up. Remove them with a slotted spoon to paper towels to drain. Repeat with remaining rice sticks. Set aside in a warm place.

Salad

1–2 C.	bib lettuce leaves
2 C.	freshly cooked chicken, cut in strips
2 T.	fresh coriander leaves
4	scallions, sliced
⅓ C.	each of the following vegetables:
	bean sprouts, blanched 1 minute in boiling water
	snow peas, blanched 30 seconds in boiling water
	bok choy or celery, thinly sliced
	small spinach leaves
	ripe red pepper, thinly sliced
	young carrot, thinly sliced

Line a bowl or serving dish with the lettuce leaves. Beat dressing to recombine and toss lightly together with chicken, coriander, and vegetables. Arrange on lettuce leaves and garnish with the crispy rice stick noodles. *Serves 4–6*

Shrimp with Hot Chili Sauce

1½ lb.	fresh shrimp
1 T.	cornstarch
2 T.	peanut oil
1 T.	minced garlic
1 slice	fresh ginger
1 T.	Panang curry base*
1 t.	sugar

---

*obtainable in Asian markets

2 strips	lime zest
	2-inch inner stalk lemongrass, chopped
⅓ C.	chicken stock
3 T.	fresh lime juice
3 T.	fish sauce
1 fresh	thin red chili, seeded and sliced (wear rubber gloves)
2 t.	sesame oil

Shell and devein shrimp, toss with cornstarch, and set aside. In a wok or a large skillet, heat oil and stir-fry the garlic and ginger for 2 minutes. Add the Panang curry base, sugar, lime zest, lemongrass, and shrimp and stir-fry for 2 minutes. Remove ginger and discard. Add the stock, lime juice, fish sauce, and red chili strips. Bring to a simmer and cook, stirring for 1 minute or until shrimp are opaque. Drizzle with sesame oil and serve. *Serves 6*

Thai Steak Salad

1	garlic clove, minced
2 T.	fresh lemon juice
2 T.	rice wine vinegar
3 T.	minced fresh mint leaves
2 T.	minced fresh lemon balm leaves
2 T.	fish sauce
2 t.	sugar
1	fresh green chili, seeded and sliced (wear rubber gloves)
6 T.	peanut oil
1 lb.	sirloin steak, cut 1-inch thick
1 T.	soy sauce
1	red bell pepper, peeled and cut in strips
6	cherry tomatoes
3	green onions, thinly sliced
3 C.	mixed salad greens

Mix together first nine ingredients to make salad dressing and refrigerate. Rub sirloin steak with soy sauce, then broil until cooked to your liking. Set steaks aside to cool for 5 minutes. Meanwhile, toss vegetables with some of the salad dressing, then arrange salad on a large platter. Slice steak thinly, arrange decoratively on top of salad, then pour two or three spoonsful of dressing over steak. *Serves 4–6*

Fresh Vegetables with Garlic and Oyster Sauce

2	T.	peanut oil
1		garlic clove, minced
2		scallions, finely sliced
1		thinly sliced baby carrot
6–8	oz.	vegetables: yellow squash, zucchini, baby corn, and snow peas
1		green chili pepper, seeded and sliced (wear rubber gloves)
4	t.	fish sauce
1½	T.	oyster sauce
2	t.	black bean sauce
2	t.	rice wine vinegar
¼	C.	chicken stock
		pinch of sugar

Heat oil in wok or large skillet, stir-fry garlic and scallions for 2 minutes. Add carrot, squash, zucchini, and corn and stir-fry until crisp-tender. Stir in chili pepper and snow peas and continue to cook for 2–3 minutes. Stir in remaining ingredients, mixing well, until simmering. Serve immediately.   *Serves 2–3*

MYANMAR (BURMA)

Myanmar, the size of Great Britain and France combined, is the biggest country in Southeast Asia. It resembles a kite with a long, flying tail. The main land mass is diamond-shaped, with a thin, coastal strip trailing along the Andaman coast to the Malaysian border. A kite is an apt analogy. Myanmar's major river, the Irrawaddy, rises in the Himalayas, flows southward for 1,350 miles (2,172 kilometers), and forms a huge fertile delta before emptying into the Andaman Sea. The Irrawaddy is a noble river, nurturing all who live near it. On its long journey, it passes through deep gorges where heavily wooded banks rise in tiers thousands of feet high. A pagoda crowns each hill. In calmer regions, villages dot the bank, their houses built of bamboo and thatch. Rice paddies cling close to the riverbank. Sickles are used to harvest the rice, and enough rice is left behind for the family water buffalo to browse upon. The rice is bound into sheaves. Bullocks tread out the grain, and it is winnowed by tossing it in a circular motion from a big woven tray. The wind whips away the chaff, leaving the grains to fall to the ground.

Water buffalo meat is eaten occasionally, though slaughtering such a hardworking animal is done reluctantly. Beef is scarce and seldom obtainable. Milk is used sparingly. The main source of protein is fish, followed by chicken, duck, and pork. To Westerners some of the foods eaten in Myanmar may seem unusual: they eat all parts of an animal—inside and out. There are no food taboos. Buddhism forbids the killing of any living thing, and this edict applies to animals slaughtered for food. Since there is no prohibition against eating meat, butchering has fallen to the Muslims and the non-Buddhist Chinese. The Chinese love pork, and have many delectable recipes for it. Accordingly, they have taken on all the butchering tasks for that particular animal, as pork is anathema to Muslims. The many rivers and lakes and the long Tenasserim coastline provide a wealth of fish. Freshwater fish is preferred to seafood. Even so, sole, red snapper, and pomfret, all from the sea, are sold increasingly at the fish markets.

Myanmar's two overwhelmingly large neighbors, China to the northeast and India to the northwest, have strongly influenced this distinctive cuisine, as has the Buddhist religion and the diverse culinary customs of the many tribal groups. China introduced the wok. The Chinese also shared their love of bean curds, soy sauce, soybean pastes, and the many different noodles—which are still eaten with chopsticks. India's contribution is evident in fresh chutney made daily, in curries scented with sweet cinnamon, cardamom, and clove, and in the wide variety of pickled foods. India invented the art of pickling over 3,000 years ago. India also brought to Myanmar the Hindu religion, which blended into the strongly held animistic beliefs held by the Myanmar people. But it was King Anawrahta, founder of the First Kingdom in 1057, who introduced Theravada Buddhism to northern Myanmar, and persuaded the people that the 37 *nats* (or spirits) they worshipped were also devout Buddhists. (Theravada Buddhism is a more conservative form of the religion that adheres to the original Pali scriptures.) Anawrahta was perhaps Myanmar's greatest king—he established a centralized government, and welded the many smaller kingdoms into one nation. He built the irrigation canals that turned the Kyaukse plain into a fertile rice granary, and introduced script to his people. Rice represents wealth in Southeast Asia. Fighting between the peoples of the region for control of the rich, rice-growing plains continued for centuries. From their stronghold in the city of Pagan, they controlled the trade routes between India and China. Anawrahta reigned for 30 years. Through conquests and the wealth they accumulated, Anawrahta built so many pagodas that the expression "as the pagodas of Pagan," synonymous with "innumerable," is still used today. Pagan became one of the most beautiful and renowned cities in the world, and is now Myanmar's major archeological attraction.

A Pagan pagoda

From 1752 to 1760, the Fourth and last Kingdom was ruled by
Alaungpaya, who built the city of Yangon (Rangoon) meaning "End
of Strife." The dynasty Alaungpaya founded ruled Myanmar until 1885
when the last monarch, King Thibaw Min, a weak and ineffective king,
was sent into exile by the British. Thibaw bankrupted the country and
unwisely imprisoned the directors of the British Bombay Burma Trade
Corporation. This act contributed to the war with Great Britain. Eventually this resulted in the annexation of the whole of Myanmar on
New Year's Day, 1886. The British ruled Myanmar for more than half
a century. After Myanmar gained its independence in 1948, semi-
autonomous states were established for some tribal groups—namely,
the Shans, Kachins, Karens, and Kayahs. Major tribal groups represent
20 percent of the population, the Burmans number 68 percent, and
the remaining 12 percent are Chinese, Indians, and a smattering of
minor tribes. The total population is about 32 million, some 3 million
of whom live in the capital, Yangon. The majority of people live in
lowland areas, working as farmers and fishermen.

Myanmar curries have the same spices as Indian curries. The
unmistakable and different taste of their curries comes from *pazun
nga-pi*, a fermented shrimp paste, and *ngapi*, fermented fish sauce.
Balachuang, a strongly flavored relish made from dried shrimp powder,
dried shrimp paste, vinegar, onions, and chili, is Myanmar's favorite
condiment, served daily with every meal. Kipling described it as "fish
pickled when it ought to have been buried long ago." Definitely an

acquired taste, it is nevertheless an essential ingredient. Discreetly mixed with other ingredients, its taste is tamed considerably. All curries are based on a slow-cooked, mellow, dense, sauce of onions, garlic, ginger, and turmeric. The main ingredient—fish, chicken, or meat—and the spices are added later. Curry powders and pastes are homemade more often than not. Small quantities of seeds, roots, herbs, and dried chilies are roasted and ground to a fine powder, the ingredients varying for each type of curry. These blends include black peppercorns, cumin seeds, dried bay leaves, cinnamon sticks, cardamom seeds, clove, coriander, and poppy seeds. The most commonly used fresh herbs are cilantro, basil, mint, lemongrass, chives, garlic chives, and onion leaves. Many kinds of wild leaves, gathered in forest and field, give a fresh taste to their foods. Curries and most other savory dishes, designed to accompany rice, are commonly spiked with hot red chilies. The less spicy Chinese curries are flavored with anise and cinnamon. Many and varied condiments and chutney, placed on the table in small dishes for everyone to share, add a wide range of flavors to food, which prevents monotony.

Dishes unique to Myanmar are hard to find outside the home. It is unusual for people to eat in restaurants. And the restaurants, most of which are in Yangon and Mandalay, serve Indian curries and Chinese noodle dishes, catering to the tastes of foreign visitors. A typical national dish is *mohinga*, a soupy mixture of noodles and fish that is eaten mainly at breakfast or at lunchtime. An ingredient

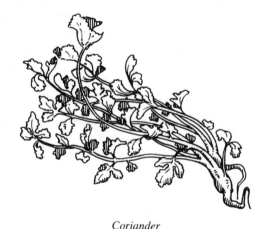

Coriander

essential to *mohinga* is sliced young banana trunk. This dish is served with tiny bowls of hot ground peppers and fresh herbs, such as cilantro, to add as desired. *Kaukswe* is another national dish, usually based on chicken with rice noodles, enriched with coconut milk. Various versions of this dish are found in different regions of the country. *Htamin Lethoke* is similar to our composed salads. The separate ingredients, set decoratively on a large platter, always include rice and potatoes. Lettuce, spinach, fresh wild leaves, assorted rice, wheat and mung bean noodles, and other cooked vegetables, round out this hearty salad. Surrounding the platter are numerous small bowls of sauces, freshly made chutney, pickles, and relishes. *Lethoke* means to mix by hand. True to its name, everyone mixes and eats this meal with their fingers. *Hingyo* is a clear soup, eaten at lunch or dinner. Specific beverages generally are not served with food, instead soup is sipped throughout the meal. Intended to freshen the palate, soups are generally light-bodied, but can be spicy, mild, or sour depending on the dishes they are designed to accompany. Homemade soup stocks, from fish heads, prawn heads, and meat bones, are extremely flavorful. Young tamarind leaves impart a sour taste to *chin hin*—sour soup. Fresh herbs, or tender, wild leaves of pumpkin, chayote, sweet pea, marigold, and acacia, are dropped in the pot at the last minute. Rice noodles are a common ingredient in soups, especially one-dish soups which are often the mainstay at dinner or lunch. Although much of Asia's food is served at room temperature, soup and rice are always served piping hot. Vegetable dishes of Chinese cabbage, bean sprouts, eggplant, bamboo shoots, and squashes and various gourds, are generally enriched with noodles.

As in most countries in Asia, mounds of rice are consumed at every meal, and no matter how elaborate and painstaking the other dishes may be, it is of prime importance to everyone gathered at the table that the rice be fluffy and fragrant. Rice is more important to many village people than the dishes served with it. Enormous value is attached to the taste, the caliber, and also the keeping qualities of rice. This is especially so among poorer families who may subsist on very little else. Affluent people supplement their vegetable curries with soybean cakes, peanut or sesame oil, and salted or fermented fish products. Many men hunt small game, and people who can afford to, raise chickens and ducks in their garden plots.

Several varieties of rice are grown in Myanmar—polished white rice, blue rice, black rice, and gluten or sticky rice used for confectionery. Long-grain rice is preferred. Some kinds absorb less water than others, depending on the variety and the age of the grain: the older the rice, the drier it is. For special occasions lemongrass is added to the pot. Little side dishes served with the rice are called *toolee moolee*. Several are strongly flavored with chili and fermented fish or shrimp sauce. Others are more benign, such as roasted chick peas, crisp bites of fried noodle, strips of fried omelettes, fried sliced onions, and crisply fried garlic cloves.

Fermented Fish Sauce: The Indispensable Condiment

Many of the dairy products we use routinely in the West to enrich our diet are not a part of Myanmar cuisine. Enrichment and savor come from fermented fish sauce, and the chunkier shrimp sauce. Over 90 percent of the people use them to enhance their largely rice diet, and they are essential to the authenticity of this cuisine. Rivers, streams, and the long coastline yield an abundance of fish and shellfish, and the Myanmar people have long evolved ways to preserve this bounty for future use. Among these are sun-drying, fermenting, pickling in brine, and salting. A variation is sun-drying fish and shrimp after they have been salted or fermented. Each has its own distinctive taste. Other foods that also are fermented, before or after sun-drying, are bean juice and bean curds. Numerous fruit and vegetable concoctions are pickled. None of these products need refrigeration. Often stored in large ceramic jars outside the house—their smell is pervasive—they can be used alone or mixed with chilies and vegetables to add zest and nutrition when meat and poultry are scarce.

A fondness for fish ensures that the banks of the Irrawaddy are dotted with fisherfolk wherever fishing is feasible. Carp, catfish, eel, and butterfish are among the hundreds of varieties of fish caught in Myanmar's teeming rivers. During the dry season, fishing huts crowd the exposed sandbanks, only to be washed away when the river swells with the monsoon rains. Near the town of Prome in central Myanmar, the fishing huts on the sandbanks are akin to a village. The fishermen

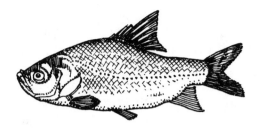

Nga thine (giant Siamese carp)

often bring their families and livestock with them and settle in for the dry season. Situated on the bank is a substantial market for the sale of *ngapi* which affords the fisherfolk a steady income from the sale of their fish. Being good Buddhists, despite their occupation, it is not unusual to see a makeshift pagoda among the huts. When asked how a good Buddhist could bring himself to kill fish, one of them replied that he didn't kill them, the fish died naturally, and if the fish were stupid enough to fall into his boat, he couldn't help that. The fishermen of the Intha people—Intha means "sons of the lake"—who live on Inle Lake in the southern part of the Shan Plateau, have an unusual and picturesque method of catching their fish. They stand with one foot on the stern of a flat boat, and use the other foot to maneuver the oar, propelling the boat over the water, as periodically they lower cone-shaped nets to snare any passing fish. The net, an ingenious contraption, is akin to a cage which works on a pivot. A rope is used to haul up the net cage. When it is raised, the fish tumble from the cage into the boat, while at the same time the water pours through the netting back into the river.

The Intha people live in stilt houses, perched on floating islands of mud and weeds, dredged from the bottom of the lake. A 3-mile-wide ring of silt, woven with water hyacinth plants and weeds, encircles the lake. It takes about 50 years to grow a meter-thick slab of this viscous mud, which can then be cut into large chunks and towed off to form islands or floating planting beds. Moored to bamboo poles thrust deep into the lake bottom, the beds are tended traditionally by women who grow eggplants, cucumbers, beans, tomatoes, and cauliflowers. Intha women are also famous for their handwoven fabric which is prized throughout the country. Farming and fishing families, living on or near Inle Lake, season their soups with the purple and white flower that grows wild around the lake. Dried and ground, one pinch will perfume a whole potful. Fond of acrid flavors, they cook with bitter-tasting gourds, and *brinjal*, hard pea-sized eggplants that retain their shape during cooking, releasing their sharp flavor only when crushed. Bitterness, they believe, improves appetite, maintains hardiness, drives out any poisons lurking in the body, and also makes the rest of the meal taste wonderful!

In mountainous tribal regions, the food is much more highly spiced than in the lowlands, and there is usually less variety. Shans, living near the Burma-China border, have a cuisine more closely related to China's than to India's. Soy sauce is used in place of fish sauce. Shans prefer dry, fried dishes, such as fried fish with soybean fritters, to eat with their soups, rather than the puréed, dense curry sauces of the lowlands. This tribe raises cattle, and their typical soup has a beef stock base. Much heavier than the light-bodied lowland versions, these soups are often thickened with soy powder, and fortified with vegetables, fungi, and leaves gathered daily in the wild. Mint and cilantro add flavor. An all-time favorite dish is hunks of smoky, three-layered pork, composed of meat, thick fat and rind, simmered with garlic, ginger, and onions.

Near Inle Lake is Taunggyi Mountain, with the Shan capital Taunggyi at its foot. The town is famous for its 5-day market, so called because the market travels daily between the five towns in the region, arriving once every 5 days. On in-between days, the market is insignificant in comparison. Booths, about 6 feet wide, line the sides of the roofed wooden enclosure, and are auctioned off to the sellers. The market enclosure at Taunggyi covers several acres. The scene shimmers with color, as much from the vendors' bright clothes as from the produce. Poorer women sit on jute sacks spread on the ground, fruits and vegetables overflowing their baskets. The fruit of the bael tree is always in evidence: the juice of this fruit is reputed to cure dysentery. This 5-day market is famed for its freshly made sweet snacks, cakes, and confections, and food counters have long lines of women, sitting on their haunches, waiting to be served. Food sellers jostle for space in the corners of the enclosure, their baskets filled with freshly cooked satays threaded on bamboo skewers and curious rice sticks that look like oversized candles. These are made from a special kind of rice mixed with water, packed into a tube of young green bamboo, and roasted in the hot ashes of a charcoal fire until the bamboo begins to crack open. When removed from the bamboo, this delicious snack retains its tubular shape.

Bright terra-cotta pots and baskets with beautiful woven designs, some big enough for a small person to hide in, make charming displays. The most curious item for sale are saucers of blossoms, picked while red ants gorge on their petals, and placed in salted water. The ants are esteemed for the sharp sour taste they give to curries and sauces. Inside the enclosure, the permanent stalls, which for security reasons can be locked at night, sell bolts of silk, handwoven fabrics, ornamental wooden combs, and graceful wooden shoes, called *pattens*. Just before New Year, fabric is much sought-after, as traditionally this is the time for everyone to have a new set of clothes, and tailors, with their treadle sewing machines, are happy to stitch up a new *longyi* on the spot. The life of the average person is largely untouched by Western influence, and, unlike their Thai neighbors, they still wear traditional dress. Men wear a cotton or silk *longyi* (similar to a wrapped skirt) with a collarless shirt. Over this is worn a short jacket called an *ingyi*. Women's clothes are similar in style but more elaborate and colorful. The ankle-length, sarong-style skirt is pulled tightly around the waist and hips. Blouses (*ingyi*) worn with them are beautifully fitted, often collarless, and generally made of silk or nylon. For women, the beauty and quality of the fabric, which is very often handwoven, is a point of pride. For formal occasions, they twist their hair into a chignon on top of their heads, decorating it lavishly with combs, jewels, or flowers. Their blouses can be very striking, especially when fastened with buttons fashioned from gold, silver, or precious gems. (Rubies, jade, sapphires, emeralds, and many other fabulous stones are mined in northern Myanmar.) The women apply cream-colored powdered bark, called *tanaka*, to their cheeks and arms. The custom may have started to protect the skin from the sun's rays. Shan people flock to Taunggyi to buy and sell their wares. The men are easy to identify by their penchant for tattoos, large striped turbans, and baggy blue trousers instead of a *longyi*. Tribal women wear jackets and elaborate headdresses, covered lavishly in silver beads, medallions, disks, and multiple silver bangles and necklaces. The family wealth is often tied up in such ornamentation. Until recently the Shans lived in feudal groups, ruled by hereditary princes.

A housewife at the market or bazaar is ruthless in her quest for the freshest fruits and vegetables. She will pry and poke, accuse the seller of hiding the best produce, dig her nails into a vegetable to assess tenderness, and turn everything topsy turvy in her quest. Oddly, no one seems to take serious offense. Vegetables, fresh and abundant, from garden or market, play a large part in every meal. Garden plots in Myanmar have most vegetables similar to those grown in the United States, and many unusual kinds, such as water spinach, long beans, winter melon, a long white radish similar to the Japanese daikon, and many kinds of gourds and squashes. Often stir-fried, vegetables are seasoned simply with a splash of soy, fish sauce, or a pinch of black pepper. Cooked salads, served at room temperature with a sprinkling of fried onions and garlic, are made with either parboiled or sautéd vegetables, dressed with oil, turmeric, and a splash of vinegar. Red chilies, fresh or dried, add fragrance and color, and act as a thickening agent in sauces. Fresh green chilies are used in salads or chutney. For recipes that simply list chili, invariably dried red chili is called for. Chilies are believed to aid digestion and sharpen the appetite. Dozens of varieties are grown and dried in the fields, then sorted by the degree of heat they impart, before being taken to market. Onions and garlic are used in great quantity. The favorite token of appreciation for dinner guests to bring with them is a 10-pound bag of garlic.

Fruits are plentiful in Myanmar and are eaten frequently as a snack and as a soothing dessert after a meal of hot curries. Limes, oranges, mangoes, papayas, pomelos (grapefruit), pineapples, and bananas are easy to find year round. Bananas, in all their bewildering variety, range from green to red in color, and from finger-sized to a yard long. Inevitably there are as many recipes for sweet snacks made with bananas as there are varieties of the fruit. They can be found sliced, rolled in flour, and crisply fried; boiled with coconut cream; batter dipped and sautéd; layered with semolina pudding; rolled in a banana leaf and steamed. The huge leaves of the banana plant are used to wrap both savory and sweet foods before steaming or grilling. The leaf imparts its own delicate flavor to the food. Leaves also substitute for plates on occasion. Slices of the tender trunk are essential to Myanmar's national dish, *mohinga*. Highly prized, delicate mangosteens, and infamous durians with their atrocious smell and wonderful taste, are grown in the south and shipped to other parts of the country.

A Celebration of Desserts

Most Myanmar have a very sweet tooth. At times of celebration or other festive occasions, when desserts are called for, the more complicated concoctions are usually purchased from commercial confectioners. Favorites are fruit pastes and preserves; diamond-shaped stiff jellies iced with coconut cream; semolina, rice, and rice noodle puddings, sweetened with palm sugar, all to be served with syrupy treacle. Cool sweet drinks are prevalent in Myanmar's steamy climate. These are made from jaggery (palm sugar) or pressed sugar cane juice mixed with coconut milk or flavored with essence of rose, mint, or pomegranate. Desserts such as sweet fritters, doughnuts, and hot steamed cakes are eaten frequently during the day as snacks.

Another essential in the diet, second only to rice, is oil. Peanut and sesame oils are produced on Myanmar's drier plains. Far larger quantities of these clear, light-colored oils are used than would suit Western tastes. On lean days, many people must be satisfied with a mound of fragrant rice, a spoonful of salt, and a bowl of peanut or sesame oil. Curry is far and away Myanmar's favorite dish, and one of its distinguishing features is the quantity and quality of the peanut or sesame oil used in the dish. When peanut oil is used, a little Chinese dark sesame oil can be sprinkled over the finished dish for additional flavor. Four ingredients essential to all curries are onions, garlic, ginger, and turmeric. The greater the quantity of onion, the thicker the finished sauce will be. Each person consumes a minimum of one pound of onions per day. For a 2–3 pound chicken, a cook would use five onions, half a fistful of garlic cloves, and one cup of oil.

Food plays an important part in Myanmar life, particularly at family celebrations and religious festivals. A typically sumptuous affair is the Sondawgyi festival, the celebration of Buddha's enlightenment. Flowered arches are raised over the streets and Chinese lanterns are hung. Dancers, puppeteers, and bands of musicians are engaged. People dance in procession along the streets, dressed in the guise of dragons, snakes, and demons. Houses are decorated inside with flags, flowers, elaborate woven fabrics, and brightly colored paper stars and rosettes. Presents for the monks are on display in the homes. Everyone dresses in their finest clothes and the women are heavily weighted with the family jewelry. The feast begins around eight o'clock. Huge mounds of steamed rice are surrounded by bowls of *ngapi*, roasts of beef and pork, heaps of dried fish, golden skinned ducks and chickens, and bowls of pickled ginger and fried garlic. Dozens of prepared dishes vie with mounds of gleaming fruits—the pick of the season—and fresh betel leaves adorn platters of betel nut. There is great enjoyment and merriment as people go from house to house, visiting friends and sampling goodies.

The biggest celebration of the year is the New Year's festival, held around March or April, depending on the astrologers. Farm laborers put down their tools, business comes to a standstill, and the government closes its doors for three or four days. Called the *Thingyan* festival, it is also known affectionately as the water-throwing festival, since everyone douses everyone else with water to wash away the old year. Not content with a water jug or a pail, trucks, equipped with full tanks and a hose, roam the streets looking for the unwary. The belief is that Thagyamin, the King of the Nats (spirits), in all his golden pomp and glory, is coming to bring good fortune for the New Year. He carries a water jar—hence the dousing—which symbolizes peace and prosperity. Floats and parades wind through the streets and guns fire in thunderous salute. Women customarily place fresh offerings at all the shrines and wash all the Buddha statues in the pagodas with holy water.

Myanmar has been aptly called the "Land of the Golden Pagodas." The most famous is the glorious Shwedagon in Yangon. Its graceful, bell-shaped stupa is a familiar site on the Yangon skyline. Completely covered in solid gold plating, it blazes in the fierce sunlight. A golden *hti* or umbrella, studded with diamonds, rubies, sapphires, and topaz, crowns the stupa. Suspended from it are tiny bells and cymbals that tinkle in the breeze. Buddhists believe that every tiny chime represents a prayer. The main stupa is surrounded by 64 smaller golden stupas. Inside the Shwedagon complex of pagodas is a treasure house and, reputedly, contains more gold than is in the vaults of the Bank of England. The wide flights of steps leading to the terraces are lined with stalls, and crowded with colorfully dressed, barefoot pilgrims.

The tourists too are barefoot as it is considered disrespectful to wear shoes in a pagoda. Stalls sell books, incense, and flowers to place at shrines, and all kinds of fascinating odds and ends for souvenir hunters.

Belief in spirits permeates Myanmar life. People walking on a dark night will sing loudly to frighten away any *nats* that may be about. The wheels of the bullock carts squeak horrendously for the same purpose. Throughout the forests of Myanmar, small wicker shrines are erected with offerings of diminutive utensils, weapons, and food to propitiate the spirits of the forests. Even the poorest village has a pagoda, and it would be rare for people not to visit one at least twice a week. Often with an attached monastery, pagodas are the social center, as well as the religious center, for the communities around them and have been for centuries. Ancient pagodas with interiors richly ornamented with lacquer work, and ornately carved wooden

Thagyamin, the king of Nats

lintels over doors and windows may still be seen. Insects and fire have destroyed a great many old structures, but, since Buddhists believe that donating the cost of a pagoda, or helping build a new one, is the surest way to earn merit for future reincarnations, pagoda-building is in full swing in all villages and towns throughout Myanmar. A newly completed pagoda, its golden umbrella encrusted with jewels (if possible), is cause for a community celebration that can last the night through, particularly if a play is performed.

Plays or dramas, called *zappwe*, are attended with enthusiasm in Myanmar. Wherever a bamboo stage is erected in the open, the whole village assembles. An orchestra, composed of several different drums, gongs, cymbals, and reed instruments, offers distraction to villagers patiently waiting for the play to begin. The plot is predictable and will be about a prince who falls in love with a beautiful commoner, or a princess wooed and won by a princely commoner. A clown, a dragon, and good and evil spirits are thrown in for good measure. Plays are always long, and usually last all night. Everyone has a great time visiting and eating together. Young mothers bring their babies swaddled in a *longyi*. Old people laugh and chat, and as the evening lengthens can be seen taking it in turns to nap, with strict instructions to waken them when a particular scene occurs. Typically, at the edge of the crowd, a haphazard market will begin to take shape. Charcoal stoves are lit, stalls erected and soon hot tea and coffee, sweet cakes, fritters, curries, rice, and a variety of snacks will be offered for sale. The lamps on the stage and the glow of the charcoal fires are often the only illumination in the dark, hot, night. The revelry continues until dawn when the brotherhood arrives with their begging bowls.

The Myanmar are all great snackers, and at any time of day will patronize food vendors hawking shrimp or peanut fritters, fried pumpkin slices, small meat or fish balls, sweetmeats, fruit, drinks, and crisps. These crisps or chips can be made from fish, shrimp, buffalo hide, fish bladders, beans, or rice. Sold at markets in dried form, they are meant to be fried before eating. A curious snack, much-loved throughout Myanmar, is pickled tea. Tender, young tea leaves, mixed with salt and sesame oil, are served to guests accompanied by tiny side dishes of roasted nuts, lentils, crisply fried sliced garlic, or dried shrimp. Packets of pickled tea accompany requests for business meetings and social invitations.

Family Life in Myanmar

Women in Myanmar are on an equal footing with men. There has never been any question of their being thought inferior to men in any way. If anything, a woman is considered less easily swayed and less gullible than her male counterpart, and a definite asset to him in negotiating business matters. Though they would never show affection for each other in public, the bond between married couples is very close. Children too share this family closeness. Women spend a great deal of time tending vegetable plots, and gathering produce for sale or for home consumption. Tasks, such as husking corn (the kernels and the husks are sold separately), drying produce, washing the family laundry usually in the nearest stream, and cooking three meals a day are time consuming. In addition women sew, weave, and may also make craft items to sell.

A typical day starts at 5 A.M. with the whole family pitching in. Children take it completely for granted that a major part of their day will be spent helping with the family chores. From quite an early age, they happily help pick vegetables, carry water, gather fuel, and babysit younger siblings. It is customary for young girls to participate in all the outdoor chores, and to prepare rice, pound spices, and make dipping sauces for the evening meal. Women are also expected to have considerable knowledge of the medicinal properties of foodstuffs, and the preparation of remedies for common ailments. Many fruits, vegetables, and leaves in the daily diet are known to possess medicinal qualities. Betel nut is one of these, and the tall, slender palm, *Areca catechu*, can be seen growing in most village plots. Just below the leaf fronds hangs a cluster of tangerine-colored fruits about the size of an egg. These are harvested before they get too ripe and then dried. The mottled whitish-brown seeds inside each fruit are boiled in water, then sliced as thin as paper. Chewing betel nut is reputed to cure aching joints and stomach pains.

Kitchens are usually rather simply equipped. Cooking is done on a portable charcoal or wood fire—generally outside the house. A grinding stone and a mortar and pestle are essential items, as is the rice grinder for making small amounts of flour. Other items are a deep, heavy iron wok with two handles (rather than one long one), sharp knives, a cleaver, a colander, a sieve, various ladles of wood or

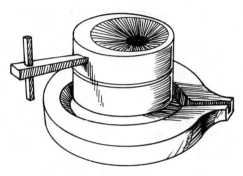

Rice grinder

bamboo, a grater for coconut meat and for grating vegetables, a long pair of tongs to move chunks of hot charcoal, a heavy round board for chopping, a wire or bamboo cage to hold meat or fish to hang outside to dry, a tiered food carrier stacked to carry items separately, and a meat safe made from wire screening, which allows air to circulate around foods, yet keeps off flies or other intruders. There will also be a low, round table, standing about 12 inches off the floor, which is the focal point of the kitchen. Women sit on low stools, or the floor, to do their food preparation. In a Western kitchen, using the food processor to make the onion, garlic, ginger, and turmeric pastes saves time and labor. An electric spice grinder is also a boon when preparing Southeast Asian foods. Time-conscious cooks may prepare curry pastes in batches and store them in airtight containers in the refrigerator or freezer. The crisply fried brown onions and garlic, used to garnish many dishes, may also be cooked in quantity and kept in the refrigerator. Since many items are used to sprinkle over rice dishes at the last minute, it is economical to be able to have them on hand, ready prepared. Not to mention the inconvenience of having the house redolent of frying onions and garlic on the day guests are expected!

Tamarind paste, made from the soft fruit of the tamarind tree, is used to impart a sour taste to dishes. The fresh young leaves, buds, and flowers are used in soups and salads. The fruit around the brown tamarind seed is light-colored when young and a darker brown when aged. The pulp is soaked in water, then rubbed through a sieve before using. The sourness it imparts is less astringent than vinegar or lemon juice. Tamarind, a hard, strong, durable wood, is used to make chopping blocks and wheels for bullock carts.

Although coconut milk and cream are mainstays in dessert recipes, they are used only occasionally in everyday cooking. Bean curds, made from lentils, split peas, and soybeans, are cooked to a soft mass, mixed with lime juice, strained through a sieve, and set aside to coagulate. Lentil curds need no cooking. Usually curds are lightly fried and added to various dishes, or crisply fried and eaten as a snack.

The various dishes served together should complement one another—a spicy hot curry with a mild or bland soup, a smooth creamy vegetable dish with crispy fried chips, sour pickles with a dish sweetened with coconut cream, and so on. A full meal for the family would generally have one condiment that is lethally laced with chili; a small bowl of pickled cabbage, a curry of fish, meat, or chicken; a stir-fried dish of vegetables flavored with shrimp, or legumes flavored with pork; a light-bodied soup with wild leaves or noodles for sipping during the meal; a salad of raw or cooked vegetables; and a pungent homemade sauce for dippers—crisp pieces of carrot, radish, cucumber, rice crackers, wild greens, herbs, and scallions. Roasted chickpea powder, diluted sour tamarind juice, and crispy fried chopped garlic, onion, and whole chilies are placed within reach for garnishing the food. A typical finale would be fresh fruit. Meals for celebrations, festivals, or guests would be more elaborate.

Myanmar too has its rules of etiquette. At the table it is customary to take only a small serving from one dish at the beginning of a meal. This is mixed with rice and eaten before another dish is tried. When all the dishes have been tasted, then it is all right to combine one or two, but never several dishes at the same time. A bowl of hot water, soap, and a towel will be placed nearby for hand washing before the meal. It is still customary to eat with the fingers of the right hand—though soup spoons and forks are sometimes provided. At the end of the meal, hand washing is again dictated by etiquette, if not by necessity.

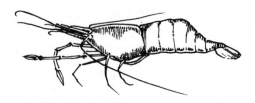

Recipes from Myanmar

Soup with Shrimp Balls and Lime

Shrimp balls

12	oz.	fresh shrimp, shelled and deveined
1	T.	fish sauce
1	T.	peanut oil
3	T.	finely chopped pork fat
1		egg white
¼	t.	salt
		pinch of sugar
		a grinding or two of pepper

Process the shrimp, fish sauce, peanut oil, and pork fat to a paste in the food processor or electric blender. Do not overprocess. Remove to a bowl, and stir in the remaining ingredients. Form into small balls; wetting your hands will help keep the mixture from sticking. Set aside in the refrigerator.

Soup

3	T.	fresh lime juice
1	T.	soy sauce
4		minced shallots
1		jalapeno pepper, seeded and minced
2	T.	whole cilantro leaves
2		scallions, finely sliced
6	C.	fish stock or clam juice and water
1		quarter-sized slice of ginger, peeled
3	T.	fish sauce

In a soup tureen put the lime juice, soy sauce, shallots, jalapeno, cilantro, and scallion. Bring the fish stock, or clam juice and water to a boil, drop in the ginger, and simmer for 1 minute. Carefully drop the shrimp balls into the simmering broth. When they become opaque, pour the soup into the tureen and serve immediately. *Serves 6*

Spiced Lentil Soup

½ C.		dried lentils
4		dried red chilies
3 T.		tamarind pulp
3 T.		peanut oil
2 medium		onions, sliced
1 T.		curry powder
2		bay leaves
4 C.		chicken stock
1 t.		salt
		freshly ground black pepper, to taste

Wash lentils and soak in water overnight. Mash lentils with a pestle. Crack chili peppers and discard seeds. Soak chilies in hot water for 10 minutes. Soak tamarind in warm water for 10 minutes, strain, and discard solids. Heat 2 tablespoons of oil in a large saucepan, add half of the sliced onion and fry until golden brown and crisp. Remove with slotted spoon to paper towels. Stir-fry the remaining onion until softened. Stir in curry powder, add bay leaves, and cook for a minute or two. Add lentils, stirring, pour in stock and bring to the boil. Lower heat and simmer for 20 minutes. Add tamarind and salt. Continue to simmer, while frying chili peppers to a dark brown in the remaining oil. Add to soup, season with freshly ground black pepper. Divide soup and chilies among four bowls, garnish with fried onions.

Serves 4

Shrimp Curry with Bean Sprouts

4		shallots
3 large		garlic cloves
1		quarter-sized slice of fresh ginger
2 small		fresh red chilies, seeds removed

½		stalk of lemongrass or 2-inch strip of lemon zest
3	T.	peanut oil
1		clove
3		cardamom pods
¼	t.	fennel seeds
½	t.	powdered turmeric
4		Italian tomatoes, seeded and diced
1	lb.	shelled and deveined shrimp
½	lb.	bean sprouts, trimmed
1	C.	canned coconut milk
1	T.	lightly chopped cilantro
1	t.	salt
2		sliced scallions
		lime wedges

Using a food processor, whirl to a paste the shallots, garlic, ginger, red chilies, and lemongrass or lemon zest. Grind in a spice grinder or a mortar and pestle the clove, cardamom seeds, and fennel seeds. Stir in the powdered turmeric. Heat the peanut oil in a wok or large skillet, stir-fry the onion paste, over medium heat, for 10 minutes or until well browned. Add ground spices and tomatoes to wok, cover, and simmer for 5 minutes. Add shrimp and bean sprouts and stir-fry for 1 minute. Stir in coconut milk, cilantro, and salt, and cook for 3 minutes, or until shrimp are opaque. Remove from heat, stir in scallions. Serve immediately with lime wedges.   *Serves 4*

Myanmar Fish Curry

2	lb.	firm, white fish fillets
1	T.	fish sauce
½	t.	turmeric
⅔	C.	oil
¼	C.	sliced onion
2		garlic cloves, chopped
1		quarter-sized slice of ginger, shredded
1	tiny	red chili pepper, seeded and sliced
2		ripe tomatoes, seeded and chopped
2		scallions, thinly sliced, for garnish

Rub fish fillets with fish sauce and turmeric. Cut fillets into 2-inch pieces. In a mini food processor, or using a mortar and pestle, make a paste of the onion, garlic, ginger, and chili pepper. Heat oil, over low heat, in a large skillet, stir-fry paste until fragrant—1–2 minutes. Add fish, turning pieces to coat with paste, cover, and cook over high heat for 2 minutes. Pour into skillet ⅓ C. water, stirring gently, then add chopped tomato and simmer, covered, for about 6 minutes. Serve garnished with scallions.   *Serves* 4

Myanmar Chicken Curry

3	lb.	chicken
1	T.	salt
½	t.	turmeric
5	or more	fresh or dried red chilies, sliced
		1-inch thick piece of gingerroot, shredded
5	medium	onions, sliced
10		garlic cloves, chopped
¾–1	C.	oil, or to taste
3		tomatoes, peeled, seeded, and diced
2–4	T.	shrimp sauce or fish sauce
1		stalk lemongrass, finely sliced
2	T.	lime juice
½	t.	ground cardamom seeds

Cut chicken breast halves in two, separate thighs from drumsticks. Rub pieces with salt and turmeric. Refrigerate. If using dried chilies, crack and shake out seeds. Soak dry chilies in water for 20 minutes. In a food processor, or using a mortar and pestle, make a paste with the ginger, half of the onions, and half of the garlic. Coat chicken pieces with paste. Heat oil over high heat, add the remaining onion and garlic. Lower heat and stir-fry until softened. Do not let it dry out. Add chicken pieces and remaining paste, stir briefly, raise heat, cover, and brown chicken. Add ½–¾ cup of water and simmer, over low heat, for 10 minutes. Stir in tomato, shrimp or fish sauce, lemongrass, lime juice, and cardamom. Cover and continue to cook until chicken is tender, golden brown, and fragrant.   *Serves* 2–3

Green Beans with Shrimp Sauce

3	thick slices of streaky bacon
¼ C.	water
2 large	shallots, chopped
2	garlic cloves, minced
1 t.	shrimp paste
2	Italian tomatoes, seeded and chopped
2 T.	fish sauce
	pinch of sugar
	pinch of salt
⅔ C.	chicken broth
½ lb.	slender green beans, trimmed

Slice bacon into strips and cook with the water in a wok until the water evaporates and the bacon just begins to crisp in the bacon fat. Remove bacon with a slotted spoon and keep warm. Stir-fry the shallots and garlic until the onion softens. Add the shrimp paste, breaking it up with a wooden spoon against the wok sides. Stir-fry for a few seconds. Stir in the chopped tomato, *patis*, sugar and salt, partially cover and cook to a thick sauce. Add broth and bring to the boil, stir in beans, reduce heat, cover, and simmer for about 8 minutes or until beans are crisp tender.   *Serves 2–3*

Chicken Breasts in Tamarind Sauce

Sauce

1½ T.	tamarind paste
1 T.	fish sauce
1 T.	rice flour
1 T.	sugar

Chicken

1 lb.	boned chicken breasts
4 t.	peanut oil
1	garlic clove, minced
½ C.	red pepper, cut in strips
¼ lb.	snow peas

1 C.   Chinese cabbage, shredded
3 T.   chicken broth
2   scallions, sliced for garnish
          whole cilantro leaves for garnish

Soak tamarind paste in one-third cup of warm water for 20 minutes, and strain liquid through a sieve. Stir in the remaining sauce ingredients, and set aside.

Cut chicken breasts into 1-inch pieces and stir-fry in a wok using half the peanut oil, over high heat for 2 minutes. Remove from wok and keep warm. Heat remaining peanut oil over medium heat, stir-fry minced garlic for 10 seconds, then add the red pepper strips and stir-fry for 3 minutes. Add snow peas and Chinese cabbage and stir-fry for 1 minute. Stir in chicken pieces, broth, and tamarind sauce. Bring sauce to boil and continue to cook, stirring for 30 seconds or until heated through. Serve sprinkled with scallions and cilantro leaves.   *Serves 4*

Tofu Stir-fried with Wild Mushrooms

⅓ C.   peanut oil
4 oz.   bean curd, cubed
2 oz.   dried shiitake, soaked for 30 minutes in warm water
1   shallot, thinly sliced
½ t.   turmeric
10 oz.   fresh wild mushrooms
1   jalapeno pepper, seeded and sliced
1 T.   fish sauce
1 T.   lime juice
½ t.   salt

Heat the oil in a wok and stir-fry the bean curd cubes. Set aside to drain on paper towel. Keep warm. Wash shiitake, discard stems, and slice. Remove all but 2 tablespoonsful of the oil from wok. Stir-fry shallot and turmeric until onion softens. Add shiitake slices, fresh wild mushrooms, halved if large, and jalapeno. Stir-fry for 2–3 minutes. Add fish sauce, lime juice, and salt and cook covered for 6 minutes. Return bean curd to the wok and stir to reheat.   *Serves 4–6*

Rich Coconut, Semolina Dessert with Sesame Seeds

⅓ C. sesame seeds
1 C. semolina or Cream of Wheat farina
1 C. sugar
1 egg
1½ C. coconut cream, fresh or canned
¼ C. corn oil
  pinch of salt
1½ C. water
½ C. chopped dates, or raisins

Over medium heat, toast the semolina in a dry skillet until light brown, watching carefully as it burns easily. Put semolina and sugar into a medium, heavy-bottomed saucepan and mix with the sugar. Beat together the egg, coconut cream, corn oil, salt, and water and pour into the dry ingredients. Let stand for 20–25 minutes. Cook mixture, stirring constantly, for 20 minutes. The mixture will be very dense and heavy. Off heat, stir in the dried fruit. Spread mixture in a shallow, heatproof dish, and sprinkle with sesame seeds. Place under broiler until sesame seeds start to color. Serve warm or at room temperature.

Serves 6–8

LAOS

Lao foods are unusual in that meat and fish are often eaten raw. Silky purées, pounded from raw meat or fish, and highly seasoned with chilies, ginger, aromatic vegetables and herbs, are wrapped in wild fresh leaves and dipped in a fiery chili sauce. Sometimes the pounded meat is mixed with finely sliced raw liver. Pounded chicken generally has thinly sliced, cooked chicken gizzards added to it. Another atypical preference of the Lao is to eat sticky or glutinous rice at every meal. Glutinous rice, in all other Southeast Asian countries, is kept for making desserts or snack foods. These intriguing creamy purées are the traditional Lao dishes served in the home. Small bowls of chopped chilies or chopped fried shallots, dipping sauces, steamed sticky rice in attractive handwoven baskets, and mounds of crisp, newly picked salad and other leaves accompany the creamy foods. Most Lao live near a forest, or at least near a wooded area, which provides a wealth of edible leaves and berries, both to decorate the table and for food wrapping. Homegrown salad leaves, assorted herbs, fennel, marguerite, lily and liana leaves, ensure freshness and incomparable flavor.

Lao food is judged by the variety of its sauces and stuffings, the degree of fineness achieved in the mincing of meat or fish dishes, the smoothness of the laboriously pounded purées, and the unique combination of ingredients to produce sauces where one or another spice or herb predominates—fennel, mint, ginger, chilies, or citrus. Variety is inherent in the different ways in which coconut is used, and in the numerous cooking methods. These may be as simple as boiling or steaming, or as complicated as the spice-laden foods, encased in clay and roasted in hot ashes. Attention to detail distinguishes the truly excellent Laos meal. Chili is by far the favorite seasoning, followed by garlic, ginger, mint, turmeric, citrus lemongrass, and onions or shallots. Pork fat is preferred for cooking, and coconut milk for its smooth texture and sweetness. Fish too is pounded to a cream and mixed with pounded vegetables. Lao fish are almost always freshwater fish from the many rivers, lakes, and streams.

Laos is a landlocked nation about the size of Wyoming, situated in the middle of mainland Southeast Asia. Alluvial soil from the 2,600-mile-long (4,184 kilometers) Mekong River enriches the floodplains, which lie between the three, sharply folded, mountain ranges that cut diagonally across the country. The Annam Cordillera separates Laos from its eastern neighbor, Vietnam. Myanmar is on Laos's northwestern border and China is directly north. The border between Laos and its western neighbor, Thailand, is formed by the Mekong River. The rich,

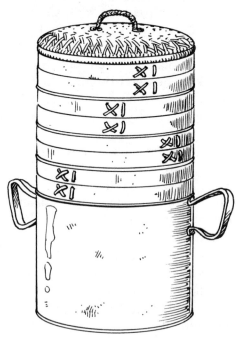

Rice steamer

black earth carried by the monsoon floodwaters provides fertile ground for the production of rice, wheat, corn, cotton, and the scores of different fruits and vegetables that play a major part in the Laos diet.

All of Laos's major towns are on the Mekong River. Vientiane, centrally located on the Laos/Thai border, is the capital of Laos. North from Vientiane is Luang Prabang. Luang Prabang is named after the Pra Bang, a three-foot-high solid gold statue of Buddha, which before 1975 was on display in the royal palace. Revered by the Laos people as a symbol of their country and their king, it has had so many squares of gold leaf pressed upon it by faithful Buddhists that its contours are somewhat blurred. The Pra Bang's whereabouts now is uncertain; it may still be within the palace compound. All that is known is that it is "secure." A spectacular Buddhist temple crowns a hill almost in the center of Luang Prabang. Intricately carved roof beams depict fierce serpents or *nagas*. Sacred to Buddhists, these creatures symbolize the mythical cobra that spread its hood over Buddha to shield him from the rain. Luang Prabang, until the communists assumed power in 1975, was the royal capital. In 1886, a French vice-consul named Auguste Pavie was appointed to Luang Prabang, and in 1887 Luang Prabang became a French protectorate. Vientiane followed suit in 1893. After treaties were negotiated between France, Siam, and Burma, the Mekong River became Laos's border. The French were ousted from Indochina during World War II by the Japanese forces. After the hostilities ceased, they returned to reclaim their colonies. But by then independence movements were astir in Laos, and in the rest of Indochina, ending in the struggle between communism and capitalism that eventually involved the Soviet Union, China, and the United States. France finally withdrew from Indochina in 1954. Communism prevailed and the Laos People's Democratic Republic was founded by the Pathet Lao in December 1975.

In the latter part of the fourteenth century, during Laos's Golden Age, the country was known as Lan Xang, meaning The Land of the Million Elephants. Elephants can still be seen today in the forests of Laos, Myanmar, and Thailand. The trained females are adept at dragging teak and rosewood logs, weighing as much as 2 tons, through the forest to the rivers, where the logs float down to a sawmill. Elephant trainers prefer females to males as they are gentle, and easier to teach. Invaluable in hilly terrain unreachable by trucks, elephants have a longer life expectancy than the machinery that replaces them and cost less in upkeep. However, at Pak Lay, the training center on the banks of the Mekong, they are unable to guarantee a sufficient number of trained elephants to meet the loggers' needs, because slash-and-burn agriculture is rapidly depleting the elephants' habitat.

The much less fertile land in the rugged mountains of Laos is not suitable for wet rice growing. Swidden, or slash-and-burn, agricultural techniques are used. Crops are planted in the nutrient-rich ashes after the land is cleared and burned. But soil is very quickly depleted, forcing the tribal people to seek new areas to burn in untouched areas of the forest. In the high mountain valleys, wet rice is cultivated. The hillsides produce dry rice, corn, wheat, cotton, and flax. Forest covers 65 percent of the country. Only about 10 percent of the land is arable. Commercial crops thrive on the Bolovens Plateau in the south. Ringed by mountain peaks, the plateau has the copious rainfall and cool temperatures needed for growing peaches, pineapples, tobacco, coffee, and a great variety of vegetables. One of the most fertile agricultural areas in Laos, during the French colonization, rubber and coffee plantations prospered here. Japan invaded Laos at the outbreak of World War II, partly to secure the rubber plantations. Some mountainous areas yield tea, tobacco, and opium. Opium cultivation is legal in Laos. The government has a monopoly on its sale, but since opium addiction is an increasing problem among the Lao, the government is trying to curtail production. The hilltribes of the Golden Triangle, where the borders of Laos, Myanmar, and Thailand meet, are subject to their own warlords, not to the central governments of the three countries involved. The largest share of the dried resin from opium is smuggled in armed caravans, controlled by hill tribesmen into Thailand.

Roughly 40 percent of the people of Laos live on or near the floodplains. The population is divided among four main ethnic groups. By far the largest group—over 50 percent—is the Lao Lum. All royalty and aristocracy came from the Lao Lum. They inhabit the lowland of the Mekong River valley. The remainder—largely people of the numerous hilltribes—populate the forested highlands. The customs of the Tai, Thueng, and Soung tribes, living in the remote upland valleys, have remained relatively unchanged. The men still wear a sarong—a long checkered cloth worn as a long skirt or wrapped to form baggy pants. Women wear patterned versions of the sarong, called a *sin*, worn with a high-necked, long-sleeved blouse, and headbands elaborately decorated with silver ornaments. Lowland Lao wear their silver around their waists.

The first people to inhabit these misty mountain valleys came from Indonesia over 10,000 years ago. Since then successive waves of immigrants, of different ethnic backgrounds and diverse cultures, from the north as well as the south, have swept into Laos. Each left its imprint on the social development and customs of modern-day Laos. Ethnically, the people of Laos are identical with their Thai neighbors. The Thais, who migrated from China's Yunnan province earlier than the Lao, settled in the Chao Phraya River basin. Today about 13 million Lao live in Northern Thailand, and the Thai hilltribes have more in common culturally, linguistically, and gastronomically with the Lao, than with their own lowland countrymen. The artificial border defining French Indochina, which was created between Thailand and Laos by the French colonists, further separated the Lao from their cousins in Thailand.

The River as Highway

There is no railroad system in Laos and roads are few. The Mekong River, the longest river in Southeast Asia, and its many tributaries, are highways for the Lao people. Goods are transported in flat-bottomed barges. Stately junks sail the broader stretches of the river. Long, slender canoes, called pirogues, navigate the rapid streams in narrow, highland waters. Sampans are everywhere. The larger ones are fishing craft, with upright poles to support nets fore and aft. Flowing from its source in the Tibetan highlands to its wide delta in southern Vietnam, the mighty Mekong River teems with fish. Ducks and other edible wildfowl throng the Mekong, which is both larder and livelihood for those who dwell on its banks.

All Lao fish and have great fun at it. Fish are caught generally for their own consumption, not to earn extra income by selling any surplus. Most of the protein in the Lao diet comes from fish, which is eaten at least twice a day. Freshwater fish predominate. There are

Pa ka gneng po (catfish)

well over one hundred varieties, among these carp, perch, and catfish. The biggest fish is the *pa beuk*—a giant catfish that lives in deep pools in the Mekong River. The *pa beuk* is much sought-after. Before the fishermen attempt to catch this giant fish, an elaborate annual ceremony is held. The spirits who guard the Mekong River are wooed with music, incantations, and offerings of incense, flowers, sweetmeats, beeswax, coconuts, betel nuts, and pieces of silver. One of these monsters can easily feed several families. The female provides at least 20 pounds of roe to be salted for *som khay*, Lao caviar. This delicacy is often served pounded to a rose-colored cream.

Lao catch not only fish and freshwater shrimp from their rivers and lakes, but also water snakes, eels, snails, and several different kinds of frog. Deep green algae, which grows on ponds, is also harvested and cooked with minced pork, eggplant, chilies, and aromatic vegetables, seasoned with *nam pa*—fish sauce. *Nam pa* is made by layering fish and salt in big vats, and steeping it until it ferments. The highly aromatic brown liquid is then drained off. This sauce is available bottled all over Laos. Indispensable throughout Southeast Asia, it is in constant use to add zest and flavor to virtually every savory dish. A similar product is *padek*, which is fish sauce with pieces of fish, rice husks, and powdered rice in it. The rice dust and husks are discarded before the sauce and its morsels of fermented fish are added to stews and similar foods. The brine, called *nam padek*, and the fish chunks may be used separately. *Padek* is generally home-made and kept in large pottery jars, usually outside on the veranda. Although strong to the Western palate, the Lao find it both delicious and nutritious. A substitute for *padek*, since it is not obtainable in America, is fermented fish imported from the Philippines.

In March, which is generally the time for plowing the rice paddies, certain species of fish migrate upriver. These migrating patterns enable the Lao to catch enormous quantities of fish at one time. Lao farmers, tilling the paddies close to the riverbank, put down lines and spread their nets. They often catch enough in one day to make a considerable quantity of *padek*. When the river is high, from May to September, a floating bait is used. The Lao have as many ingenious ways to catch fish as there are varieties. The hill people prefer small nets, lines and poles in their fast-running mountain streams. In October, in the valleys, dams are built in the riverbeds to trap the fish as they return downstream. This practice nets from 130 to 260 pounds of fish in one day, most of which is then fermented. Each family uses between 90 and 110 pounds of *padek* per year for their protein needs when fresh fish is not obtainable.

Little can be done to dam the swift waters of the Mekong River. Subsiding waters may leave small pools on some wide, sandy stretches of the Mekong, which trap young fish and yield an easy catch. The farmers who live too far from a river to make fishing a daily occupation often band together with their neighbors and go on fishing expeditions. Shouts of delight are heard up and down the river as people emerge from the water with a wriggling fish. Occasionally someone might decide to sell off some of the extra fish at the local market, but almost always surplus fish are preserved for later use. Some inland villages build their own ponds, and stock them. Very large lakes may have a plant where fish are dried for shipment to other regions of the country, or processed into *nam pa.*

Villages invariably are situated by a stream or a river, often fed by rivulets from the dense wall of jungle, which is never far away. Typically the streams and canals are shaded by coconut palms and mulberry trees, both essential to village life. The coconut palm is invaluable, providing not only rich white meat from the nut—which in turn yields coconut milk and cream used in so many recipes—but

Pa hang fa, often grilled

also dried coconut meat, called copra. Potentially, this is an important export product. Coconut oil, from processed copra, is prized in developed nations for use in food processing. The husk of this useful plant provides strong fibers for rope and matting, and the leaves are used by villagers and hilltribe people to make woven baskets. Mulberry leaves feed silkworms. Villagers spin and weave their own clothing and, using the delicate silk produced by their carefully tended silkworms, weave fine silk goods to sell. Black dikes, needed for irrigation control, criss-cross the level land between the rivers and streams.

Above the floodplain and the rice paddies, houses perch on log pilings 8 feet (7 meters) high. Built of woven bamboo poles with thatched roofs, a ladder or steps lead up to the communal veranda, which runs the length of the rectangular house. Cooking is usually done on the veranda. It also provides extra sleeping space. The walls dividing the space inside do not reach to the ceiling, allowing air to circulate more freely. Behind the veranda is the family room, which also runs the length of the house. Here is the family hearth, and the all-important family altar. All significant family ceremonies are held before this altar, which may be dedicated to any of the many spirits. When the ladder is pulled up onto the veranda for the night, the last rung is left poking over the edge for the spirit who guards the house to sit upon. Bamboo screens roll down for protection against rain. Sleeping rooms, equipped with mats for sleeping, lead off of the family room. Shelves and baskets provide storage for clothes and personal belongings. A table and a few chairs may be the only furniture. Most village houses have a barn outside for their animals. The family water buffalo is indispensable. It pulls the plow in the rice paddies, drags heavy soil for building and repairing dikes, and also pulls the farmer's wagon. It is a man's task to fish, hunt, plow the paddies, and build boats, wagons, tools, and other necessities. Women spin, weave, clean, cook, and tend the garden. It is also a woman's task to sell any surplus produce at the market. Cooking is heavy work, as it involves toting water from the river or well and carrying wood for the charcoal stove. During planting season, grandmothers look after the children while younger women help transplant the rice shoots. Every able-bodied person pitches in as rice literally sustains them. Children, as soon as they are able, help in the garden and tend the animals.

Almost all Lao living in rural areas have neither electricity nor plumbing in their houses. People bathe daily in the rivers. Portable charcoal or kerosene stoves are used for most cooking. Grilling usually takes place outside on a wood-burning stove, rather like a campfire, which has several stones arranged to shelter the fire, and support the metal grill. Meat and fish, coated with clay, or securely wrapped in dampened tree bark, are cooked in the hot ashes of a wood-burning stove. Cooking methods are simple yet inventive, and all foods, whether trapped, fished out of the nearest stream, or grown in the family plot, are absolutely fresh. Most Lao are subsistence farmers, growing only enough for their family's needs, as there are few adequate roads to take surplus goods to market. The coconut palm, the betel palm, and banana plants are grown commercially in villages and on plantations. The betel palm yields a nut that is mildly narcotic. Thin slices of betel nut are chewed all over India and Southeast Asia, staining lips, gums, and teeth a brilliant red.

The Lao are expert craft makers. Their carving skills are well known, as is their expertise in making beautiful pottery, leather and metal goods, and stunning lacquer ware. Weaving and tapestry work produce high-quality goods both in highland and lowland areas. Baskets, made from rattan and other fibers, are exported to Thailand. Lao villagers are self-sufficient, which not only instills a sense of pride, but also ensures survival when times are bad. Money is necessary for buying salt, and for kerosene to light lamps and to burn in their stoves.

The Cuisine of Laos

Beef is hard to find in Laos, and what little is accessible is prohibitively expensive. Water buffalo, a much-loved substitute, is cooked in countless recipes, and also pounded to a paste and enjoyed raw. Dried water buffalo skin is a frequent ingredient in Lao cooking, as is fried pork skin. Pork is very popular in Laos. Most villages will have a pig or two about the place. Not only is it an economical animal to raise, since it generally forages for itself, but all parts of the animal, from its head to its trotters, are edible. Three-layer-pork, comprising skin, fat, and lean meat, is sold in slabs. Lao cooking would not be

Lao cooking without three-layer-pork. Dried buffalo skin, fried pork skin, three-layer-pork, and spit-roasted pork may all be purchased ready to use in Lao markets.

Poultry is held in high esteem by everyone—the gizzards in particular are considered a great treat. Both chickens and ducks are raised on family plots. In the poorer regions of Laos, where it is not always possible to produce enough food for each day's needs, hunting is a necessity. Wild deer, called *fahn*, wild chicken, and tiny game birds such as quail, are much sought after. Eggs are used very rarely in Lao cooking. Most people prefer to wait for the chicks to hatch. Desserts at festival time prove the exception. *Sang khaya mak u*, a custard steamed inside a seeded pumpkin shell, is rich in eggs and coconut milk. *Foy Thong* is a dessert made by cooking threads of beaten egg in sugar syrup, and *khanon mo keng* is a mixture of sugar, eggs, and onions. *Phan khay*, pancakes made with a rich egg batter, are stuffed with raw meat, then wrapped in banana leaves and steamed. Eggs, which connote fertility, are a frequent part of animist ceremonies.

Some of the vegetables in common use are yams, pumpkins, cucumber, kohlrabi, cabbage, mushrooms, french beans, long beans, bean sprouts, sweet peppers, and many varieties of radishes and gourds. The use of edible leaves to wrap foods, endless amounts of which are gathered daily from gardens, riverbanks, and forests, is one of the things that distinguish Lao cooking. Almost all Lao households have a garden where *phak salat* (lettuce), cabbages of various kinds, spinach, small round eggplants, avocado, cassava, spring onions, many different varieties of hot chilies, myriad herbs, lemongrass, shallots, ginger, and a banana plant or two are grown. Delicious wild fungi are also collected daily, all of which contribute freshness, intriguing textures, and great flavor to their dishes. Cooked vegetables are never served as a separate dish, but are used to augment a particular dish, or to enrich soups or salads.

Fruit is plentiful, fresh, and luscious. These include pear, mango, lime, guava, mandarin orange, watermelon, rose-apple, pineapple, grapefruit, longan, papaya, custard-apple, the prized, delicate mangosteen, the hairy red rambutan, durian, with its foul smell and incomparable flavor, jackfruit, and banana. Bananas range from creamy yellow through deep red to green in color and they can be as small as a finger or as long as an arm. Bananas also provide leaves to wrap

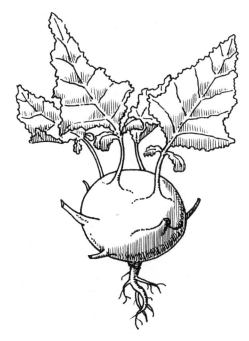

Kohlrabi

foods to be steamed or grilled. The tender flower bud and the delicate inner trunk enhance several recipes. Banana flower buds are obtainable canned from the Philippines in Asian markets in America. The flower of the ginger plant is also an ingredient in Lao dishes. Fruit is usually eaten at the end of a meal. Desserts served when guests arrive could include coconut custard, bananas in coconut milk, sticky rice in coconut cream with ripe mango, or sticky rice cakes. Everyone's favorite dessert is coconut-laced, sticky rice roasted in a bamboo tube.

Mixing fish and meat in sauces and soups is commonplace in Laos. Despite the fact that this is a Chinese custom, as a general rule, Lao cooking is less influenced by the cuisine of China than by other Southeast Asian countries such as Malaysia, Thailand, and India. Blending sweet and sour ingredients in the same dish, a typical feature of Chinese cuisine, is not part of the Lao repertoire. Indian spices perfume Lao curries. Sumatrans and Thais are well known for their predilection for scorchingly hot food, and the predominant flavor in Lao food is also the fiery chili pepper. Used with gusto, it is found in almost every dish. Typically in Lao recipes, each ingredient is fried separately, usually in lard, and set aside until needed. Fried onions, garlic, and shallots are typical garnishes.

Chinese people have been migrating to Laos for hundreds of years. Over 50 percent of them live in Vientiane. Astute businessmen, they dominate banking and some industries. Hotels, cinemas, and restaurants in Vientiane are all owned and run by Chinese, as are jewelry stores and most repair shops. Pakistanis and Indians, more visible minorities than the Chinese, also prefer city living. Tailoring and fabric stores in the capital are generally owned by Indians. Vientiane has several open-air markets. The most famous are the Morning market and the Evening market—though, curiously, both are open all day. The Morning market sells fresh flowers, fresh vegetables, fresh meats, and also fabrics, jewelry, hardware, pots and pans, tobacco, ready-made clothes, and innumerable odds and ends. The Evening market, the larger of the two, sells much the same goods. Foodstalls in the markets specialize in well-cooked Lao dishes, and there are one or two small restaurants serving European-style Lao food.

Genuine Lao food is not available in restaurants. It takes too long to prepare and is too labor-intensive. The majority of the restaurants

Kanab (food wrapped in banana leaf)

serve Chinese or French cuisine. An exception is an establishment that will prepare Lao dishes with 24 hours' notice, but for the most part, authentic Lao food is available only in the home. People rarely go to restaurants. Nightlife in Vientiane is nonexistent, though recently young people seem to be gravitating toward disco music. France has left its mark on the culture and cuisine of Laos. Roast chicken, French potato dishes, French wines, and in particular, French bread are very much a part of Lao cuisine. Baguettes and pastries are readily obtainable in the cities of Vientiane, Luang Prabang, and Savannakhet. Vendors sell baguettes for breakfast, split and stuffed with a concoction similar to our cold cuts. There are many noodle shops in the cities, mostly in the Chinese section, specializing in noodle soup, and the ever-popular fried noodles, enlivened with bits of meat or fish.

Vientiane is the site of *That Luang*, a sixteenth-century Buddhist shrine, near the former royal residence. The shrine has some of the best remaining examples of carved teak in the country. The tropical climate and wood-boring insects have destroyed much of this fine craftsmanship over the centuries. Buddhism and animism exist side by side in Laos, except for the hilltribes who practice only animism (spirit worship). Prayers and supplications to the spirit world are a daily practice, despite strong discouragement from the ruling communist regime. Spirit worship stems from the belief that nonliving objects possess a living spirit, and, unless it chooses to manifest itself, it remains invisible. Rocks, water, wind, forests, trees, land, crops— even the wood used to build a house—has its own living spirit. Some spirits are good, some not. This belief gives immense meaning to practically anything that happens in life—from happy coincidences to major disasters, such as earthquake or fire. There is a hierarchy of spirits. The major ones are believed to control harvests and each person's good or bad fortune each year. Minor spirits are the domain of sorcerers who are consulted frequently to prevent disasters or to predict the future. Astrologers decide the most auspicious dates for important occasions. Far-reaching taboos govern the lives of tribal people, and infringements are severely punished. Great care is taken when choosing a site for a house, a paddy field, or a burial ground, and it is commonplace to see shrines or altars beside water, woods, or rice fields.

An important spirit ceremony, openly practiced despite the government's taboo, is *baci* or *sukhuan*. *Sukhuan* means to welcome the soul, or to ask the soul to return to the body. The Lao believe that the soul has a wandering nature, and on occasion leaves the body. No Lao would leave on a journey without holding a *baci* first. *Bacis* are held for a wedding, a newborn child, for New Year, to speed recovery from an illness, or simply to welcome friends back after a long separation. *Baci* ceremonies take place around a 2–3-foot-high cone of flowers. This is made from a section of banana plant trunk, imbedded in an upright position, in a large bowl of dry rice, and decorated with masses of fresh flowers. Its shape resembles a small Christmas tree. Placed on a low table, guests sit around the "flower tree" on the floor. String, which symbolizes good fortune, is wrapped around the tree. Special foods appropriate to the occasion are arranged nearby. For example, eggs denoting fertility would be served at a wedding *baci*. Almost certainly there would be the two forms of ginger, regular ginger and zingiber zerumbet, which represent gold and silver in the spirit world. A village elder will pray to the spirits for whatever the person giving the *baci* requests. After the incantations, guests come forward and tie cotton strings to the wrist of the person who is being honored. Everyone in turn receives a lucky thread. These are supposed to remain tied around the wrist for three days, but most people leave them there until they drop off.

The ruling regime forbids monks to encourage spirit worship. Along with their Buddhist training, monks now undergo political indoctrination. Nevertheless, Buddhism is still an important social force. The Lao's basic philosophy and their values derive from Buddhism—respect for elders, generosity, sensitivity to the feelings of others, an even temper and polite decorum, all hail from Buddhism. The Lao are graceful and gentle, and although life is hard for them, and their daily chores onerous, they are basically a lighthearted people, and find many occasions to enjoy themselves. It is not in the Lao nature to work full time, in order to accumulate money in excess of daily needs. Much rejoicing and delight herald the festival days, which are studded throughout the Lao lunar calendar. New Year is a three-day public holiday. The celebration, depending on astrological signs interpreted by the monks, begins around April 15. Food always plays a big part in these festivities. For days in advance, much chopping and pounding is heard as the women throughout the village prepare dishes and delicacies to share. Everyone cleans house to rid them of malign spirits, and clothes are refurbished in preparation for the festivities. Offerings for prosperity in the coming year are placed before family altars, and images of the Buddha in the *wats* are sprinkled with holy water. Holy images, floats, and a procession of masked participants usher out the old year. During the holidays, anyone walking on the street is likely to be unexpectedly doused with water to wash away the sins of the old year. Urchins throw bucketfuls upon the unwary. In the evenings, musicians and troupes of dancers stroll from village to village beneath trees strung with lanterns, and people continue to celebrate far into the night.

Festive Dishes and Family Fare

A much-revered festival dish is *lap*. Expensive to make, it is a great luxury. The main ingredient in *lap* is raw buffalo meat, pounded to a smooth cream. The very thinly sliced buffalo liver is gently stirred into the dish, along with minced garlic, shredded ginger, chilies, roasted eggplant, and roasted, powdered glutinous rice. The final assemblage is served with lime juice, fish sauce, sliced scallions, several kinds of chopped mint, garden-fresh leaves for wrapping portions of *lap*, and a hot condiment for dipping the leaf-wrapped packages. Lao cooks create variety of taste and texture in their meat stews, fish dishes, and sauces by blending tart and acidic flavors with wild, strongly aromatic leaves.

Khao poun is a festival dish of rice vermicelli, cooked in coconut milk, with a sauce that combines fish and meat. Another party dish is whole chicken, stuffed with peanuts and spices, simmered in coconut milk. A variation of Mongolian hot pot, called *phalam long*, is great fun to share with friends. Each person cooks his or her own thinly sliced, raw meat, in a hot flavorful broth, and wraps the meat with rice vermicelli and fresh greens. The sauce for this dish is usually a richly flavored peanut sauce. Small cakes of pounded fish, called *mok pa*, steamed in banana leaves are common at festivals. Tiny, creamy white or pale green striped eggplants are regularly pounded with fish for puréed dishes. Pork, pork liver, the heart, and a small portion of

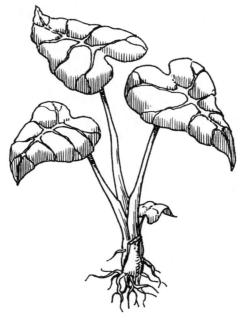

Giant taro leaves

dried rind are pounded, then seasoned lavishly with chilies and on-ions, to make *sa mu*. One of the best-loved foods in Laos is a pickled sausage, called *nam*, made from raw pork loaded with spices and garlic, served with yet more blistering, tiny chilies, ginger, peanuts, and scallions. It keeps for a day or two without refrigeration, preserved by the garlic and chilies.

Lao women seem quite content to spend long hours preparing their traditional dishes. Fish and chicken are almost always served boned. All the pounding, mincing, chopping, and slicing is done while seated on the floor, and with the extended families common in Laos, there are almost always two or more women tackling these chores together.

Glutinous rice is eaten three times a day, steamed in a basket over boiling water. These individual lidded baskets are intricately woven in pleasing patterns. For breakfast, glutinous rice is soaked overnight, steamed, and flavored with *nam padek* or served with fruit, black beans, or yams. Popular at breakfast is a noodle soup, called *furr*, which is served topped with bits of pork, garlic, and, surprisingly, marijuana leaves. Big bunches of marijuana are readily accessible in the markets, as in Laos it is considered simply an herb. Each of the Southeast Asian countries has its own recipe for *furr*. In Laos it contains a lot of vegetables and sometimes peanut sauce, in Vietnam it would contain meat. A Lao pleasantry is that a *furr* shop that suddenly gets crowded is adding more marijuana to its noodles! Lunch frequently consists of soups fortified with pork or bean curd, or enriched with fish, mushrooms, and spices. Noodle or rice dishes with morsels of fish or meat are eaten often at lunchtime. But whichever dish is chosen, it will always be enlivened with hot sauce.

Dinner is steaming hot, glutinous rice, surrounded with an assortment of small, cooked dishes and a platter of salad. Fermented pork and fish dishes, made by pounding the food with fermented rice, as

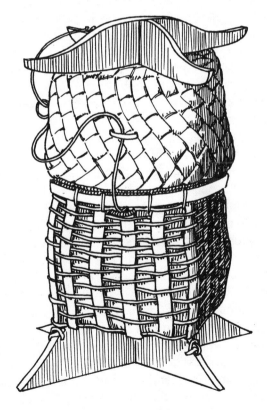

Rice basket

well as salted and dried foods, appear fairly frequently on a Lao table. These foods are preserved when the harvest is abundant. Lao meals always include soup, either to end the meal or to sip during the meal to refresh the palate. It is never served alone as a first course. Fish- or meat-based soups are varied with additions of mushrooms, cabbage, or bamboo shoots, and may be spicy or mild depending on the dishes they are to accompany. Dried buffalo skin is added to plain vegetable soups for flavor. Dried or roasted rice, pounded to a powder, acts as a thickening agent where needed. Green papaya salad, spiked with fresh chilies, is eaten with gusto all over Southeast Asia. The range of flavors and textures from the many herbs, roots, and vegetables gathered each day ensures that the meals are never monotonous.

The Lao will often happily sip a cup of hot water during a meal. Pale Chinese tea, hot or iced, is also served, as is coffee—particularly at breakfast. Alcoholic drinks are accessible. Government breweries produce three kinds of beer. Other beers are imported from Singapore and Australia. Two brands of rice whiskey are distilled by the government brewery, and these are usually spliced with lime juice and a splash of soda. Some village households ferment their own version of rice whiskey. Orange soda and Coke, imported from Thailand, are also readily obtainable.

Rules of etiquette govern behavior at a Lao table. For example, guests may not eat until the host has invited each person to start eating. They must never reach for a dish at the same time as anyone else, especially if that person is elderly or has a higher social position. A guest cannot continue eating if everyone else has finished, and it is essential to leave some food on the plate, to give the impression that more was offered than could be consumed. Hospitality dictates that more places be set at table than the number of guests who are expected, and the lavishness of the food served guarantees plenty of leftovers. There are rules to be followed even when eating en famille. Each family member serves himself according to age, starting with the eldest adult and continuing on down, until the youngest person has taken a helping. Then everybody is free to eat in any order, bearing in mind the rule dictating that no two people may take food from the same dish at the same time, and that they defer to people of higher rank. Etiquette demands that the lid be replaced on each rice basket as soon as the person has finished eating. Rice is much more expensive than other foods, and far more costly in Laos than it is in countries that have wider rice-growing plains. Served sparingly at a Lao table, much more emphasis is placed on the two or three other dishes that accompany the rice. These dishes are not eaten, as in Thailand, simply as condiments, but are the foundation of the meal. Fish dishes are served frequently, and very often the meat or fish will be served raw. Balls of sticky rice, lightly kneaded with the fingertips, are used to mop up sauce and to maneuver food around the plate. Spoons are used for soups and dishes with a liquid consistency. Chopsticks are used only for noodle dishes.

Chopping and pounding are the main methods used in the preparation of Lao cooking. Chopping is usually done with a heavy knife on a stout block of wood cut from a tree trunk. A strong cleaver would also be found in a Lao kitchen. A mortar and pestle is used for pounding. Dried herbs, dried chilies, and roasted or dried rice are pounded to a fine powder. When large quantities of rice flour are needed for baking, a hand-turned rice mill is used. Equipment for the kitchen would include a steamer, consisting of a rounded pot for boiling water with a wide neck, supporting a lidded bamboo rice basket. Chinese steamers, in use in Lao kitchens, consist of a stack of circular bamboo containers, fitting one on top of the other, permitting the steam to rise through all the layers. This enables different foods to be kept separate yet steamed all together. Each family has a large ceramic or metal pot for soup, and a heavy iron, general-purpose cooking pot with a lid. A wok, which is used throughout Southeast Asia, is an essential utensil. Coconut husks double for ladles and small general-purpose bowls. Strainers or sieves are made from bamboo, as are the highly decorative woven baskets used as individual containers for serving sticky rice. Any well-equipped American kitchen will have the tools needed to prepare Lao foods.

Recipes from Laos

Fish Ball Appetizers

1 lb.	white fish fillets, finely chopped
2 T.	fish sauce
½ t.	salt
4	fresh chili peppers, finely sliced

I	large	shallot, finely minced
2		stalks of lemongrass, finely sliced
6		garlic cloves, pressed
½	C.	grated coconut
2		scallions, chopped
2	T.	Chinese parsley, minced
I		egg white, beaten
2	T.	rice flour
		oil for frying

Toss minced fish with fish sauce and salt. Place in a mixing bowl. Pound or purée in a food processor the chili peppers, shallot, and lemongrass. Mix the paste with the pressed garlic, coconut, scallions, and parsley. Add the beaten egg white and the flour to the fish mixture and thoroughly blend in the paste ingredients. Form into one-inch balls, and fry in hot oil until golden brown.

Serves 3–4

Lao Fish Soup with Lime

3	C.	flavorful fish stock OR
		clam juice diluted with water
I-lb.	can	Italian tomatoes, puréed
I	t.	salt (optional)
I		whole inner stalk of lemongrass, lightly pounded
I	lb.	boned trout, sliced into 2-inch strips
I		tiny, fresh green chili, seeded and sliced (wear rubber gloves)
3	T.	fish sauce
8–12		button mushrooms
2	T.	fresh lime juice
		green part of 6 scallions, thinly sliced
I–2	T.	fresh, whole coriander leaves

Pour fish stock or equivalent, tomatoes, optional salt, and whole lemongrass stalk into a large saucepan. Bring to the boil and simmer, uncovered, for 15 minutes. Remove and discard lemongrass. Add fish, green chili, fish sauce, and button mushrooms. Bring to the boil and simmer, over low heat, for 6 or 7 minutes, depending on thickness of fish. Add lime juice and remove from heat. Serve garnished with sliced scallions and coriander leaves.

Serves 6

Steamed Chicken Stuffed with Peanuts

	juice of one lime
2	dried red chili peppers
	seeds from 6 cardamom pods
1 t.	fennel seeds
½ t.	salt
3–4 lb.	roasting chicken, fat removed
1 T.	peanut oil
1 medium	onion, chopped
4–5 oz.	loose pork sausage
1 C.	toasted peanuts, chopped
3–4	dried red chilies, toasted and ground
3 T.	fresh lime juice
1 T.	minced fresh mint leaves
6	mint leaves, for garnish
½ t.	soy sauce

In a spice grinder or mortar and pestle, grind the dried chili pepper, cardamom seeds, fennel seeds, and salt. Set aside spice mixture. Heat peanut oil in medium-sized skillet and stir-fry onions until lightly browned. Add crumbled pork sausage and stir until no longer pink. Remove from heat and stir in peanuts, toasted ground chili peppers, one tablespoon of lime juice, and chopped mint. Place stuffing in cavity of bird and skewer closed. Place chicken in a shallow heatproof dish and pour remaining lime juice over it. Rub reserved spice mixture all over chicken. Place dish in a large steamer over rapidly boiling water. Cover and steam chicken until juices run clear when pricked with a fork—about 50 minutes—replenishing water as needed. Remove chicken to a serving platter and keep warm. Pour juices into a sauce-boat, skim off fat, and season juices with soy sauce. Serve chicken, garnished with mint leaves, and pass the pan juices separately.

Serves 6

Beef and Vegetable Stew

¼ lb.	fresh pork fat, cubed
2 large	shallots, minced
5	garlic cloves, minced

1 lb.		sirloin or rump steak, sliced into strips
3 T.		fish sauce
3		carrots, peeled and diced
4		wild mushrooms; if dried, soak in warm water for 10 minutes
1 small		can bamboo shoots, drained
½ lb.		fresh water chestnuts, peeled and sliced
4		ripe tomatoes, seeded and diced
1 C.		beef broth
2		eggs
3		scallions
1 T.		minced Chinese parsley
1 t.		fish sauce
1 t.		sesame oil
¼ t.		freshly ground black pepper
		salt to taste
		whole coriander leaves

In a large saucepan, render the pork fat, strain and discard solids, and return fat to pan and reheat over medium flame. Sauté the shallots and garlic for 2–3 minutes, raise heat slightly, add the beef, and stir to sear evenly. Lower heat to medium, add the 3 tablespoons of fish sauce, diced carrots, sliced mushrooms, bamboo shoots, water chestnuts, diced tomatoes, salt, and beef broth. Simmer for 20–25 minutes, uncovered. Do not let it dry out. Meanwhile beat two eggs in a small bowl, add the Chinese parsley, the teaspoon of fish sauce, and minced scallion greens from one of the scallions. Heat one teaspoon of sesame oil to coat a small skillet, pour in egg mixture, tipping skillet to form a flat sheet of egg. Cover and cook until egg is set. Turn out onto a board or plate. When cool, roll up and slice. When beef is cooked, add freshly ground pepper and salt, if needed. Pour into a heated serving dish and garnish with omelette strips, coriander leaves, and the remaining scallions sliced.   *Serves 3–4*

Spicy Fish Purée with Wrapping Leaves and Dipping Sauce

2½ lb.		white-fleshed, fresh fish
1		head of garlic

6		Japanese eggplants OR I large eggplant
2		shallots
¼	lb.	rice vermicelli, soaked in hot water for 10 minutes
2	T.	fish sauce
3		fresh, hot red chilies, seeded and sliced
3	T.	chopped fresh mint
I	T.	chopped fresh coriander

Dipping sauce

I		fresh red chili pepper, seeded and minced
4	T.	fish sauce mixed with 2–3 T. water
3	T.	lime juice
I	t.	sugar
		pinch of salt

Salad leaves

	Red leaf lettuce
	arugula
	Boston lettuce
2	scallions, cut in long slivers
	sprigs of chervil
	basil leaves
	coriander sprigs

Grill fish over charcoal until well-done. Set aside to cool. In a 375°F oven, roast eggplants, shallots, and the head of garlic until the skins are charred and the insides soft. Cool. Drop soaked vermicelli in boiling water for I minute. Drain and chop roughly. Debone and flake fish. Remove skin from roasted vegetables. In a food processor, purée the fish with the eggplant, shallots, fish sauce, chilies, mint, coriander, and half of the garlic. Stir vermicelli into the purée and place in a serving bowl.

To make the dipping sauce, purée the rest of the garlic with the chili, stir into the remaining sauce ingredients. Heat the dipping sauce ingredients briefly, and cool. Serve the fish and eggplant purée surrounded with the salad leaves and herbs for wrapping, and the dipping sauce on the side. *Serves 6*

Steamed Shrimp in Banana Leaf Packets

	banana leaves or aluminum foil for wrapping
2 lb.	shrimp, peeled and deveined
1 t.	salt
2 small	red chili peppers, minced
3	shallots, finely sliced
1 t.	very finely shredded ginger
2	inner stalks of lemongrass, finely sliced
2 T.	fish sauce
8	basil leaves
2 T.	minced coriander
	lime wedges

Banana leaves should be soaked in boiling water to soften them. Drain and clean with a damp cloth. Cut into 10-inch squares and patch, where necessary, with extra leaves.

Toss the shrimp with the salt and set aside. Pound, or process, the chili peppers, shallots, ginger, and lemongrass to a paste. Mix in the fish sauce and lime. Add to the shrimp and toss well to coat shrimp with paste. Divide in four and place on four banana leaves. More than one leaf will be needed for each packet as they frequently need to be overlapped where they are torn. Wrap securely and fasten with a piece of bamboo. Place in a steamer and when the water boils, steam packets for 20 minutes. Put the packets on four warmed plates. Serve with tiny bowls of fresh herbs for garnishing and lime wedges.

Serves 4

Catfish and Vegetable Stew in Coconut Milk

2 lb.	catfish fillets, cut into 2-inch chunks
1 t.	salt
1 t.	galangal, or fresh ginger, finely shredded
2	shallots, thinly sliced
2	garlic cloves, minced
2	fresh hot green chilies
1	inner stalk of lemongrass, shredded
2 T.	peanut oil

1 T.	dried shrimp paste
4 small	Japanese eggplants, stems removed and thickly sliced
2 C.	cauliflower florets
1 C.	tender carrots, sliced
3 T.	fish sauce
2 cans	coconut milk
1 C.	watercress leaves
4	Kaffir lime leaves, vein removed and leaves thinly shredded
	cilantro leaves
	lime wedges

Toss the fish with the salt and galangal. Set aside. In a mini food processor, make a paste with the shallots, garlic, chilies, and lemongrass. Heat the oil in a wok, and stir-fry the shrimp paste, breaking it up against the side of the pan. Add the paste, and stir-fry until fragrant. Put the fish pieces in the wok and continue to stir-fry for a minute or two. Remove fish with a slotted spoon and keep warm. Stir into the wok the eggplants, cauliflower florets, and carrots to coat with mixture. Pour in the fish sauce and coconut milk and cook for about 10 minutes or until vegetables are tender. Return the fish to the wok with the watercress leaves and the Kaffir lime leaves. Cook for 2 or 3 more minutes. Sprinkle with the cilantro leaves and serve with the lime wedges. *Serves 4*

Dried Meat from Heaven

In Laos the beef is dried in the hot sun in a net cage, to discourage predators, for a day. It can be made successfully in a gas oven with a lighted pilot flame burning, but an electric oven is not suitable as it is impossible to keep the heat low enough.

2–3 lb.	sirloin or rump roast
2 t.	salt
1 t.	freshly ground black pepper
3 t.	sugar
1 T.	coriander seeds, crushed
1–2 T.	dark Chinese sesame oil
3	garlic cloves, pressed
1 T.	peanut oil

Trim off any fat and slice beef into ⅛-inch-thick strips of equal thickness. This is important for even drying. Mix all ingredients thoroughly and marinate for at least 3 hours, or refrigerate overnight. Arrange meat on racks, spaced so air can circulate, and place in a gas oven with the pilot light lit for 10–12 hours, with the door closed. Or, if possible, dry meat in the sun, turning once during the drying process. Beef strips should be removed as they dry to an airtight container, where they will keep for 3 weeks. Beef can also be frozen for up to 9 months. Strips can be broiled briefly to enhance flavor before serving.

Lap—A Traditional Festival Dish of Raw Chicken Purée

1		3-lb. chicken, skin, liver, and gizzard reserved
½	C.	chicken broth
4		Japanese eggplants
2		shallots
2		heads of garlic
4	small	dried red chili peppers
2		thick slices of fresh ginger
2	t.	salt
3	C.	chicken broth
½	C.	fish sauce
1	T.	shrimp paste
¼	C.	toasted ground uncooked rice
¼	C.	fried garlic slices
		juice of 1 large lime
		Garnishes: minced cilantro leaves, chopped scallions, Kaffir lime leaves, finely sliced
		Salad leaves, mint, basil, cilantro, fennel leaves, thin carrot sticks, radishes, and garlic chives

Bone chicken and finely mince, or briefly process, chicken meat. Cook skin, liver, and gizzard in chicken broth, until tender. Cool, mince finely, and add to chicken. Refrigerate. Roast eggplants, shallots, heads of garlic, chili peppers, and ginger. When cool, pound or process roasted vegetables with the salt. Bring one-half cup of chicken broth to the boil and stir in fish sauce. Dissolve shrimp paste in hot broth. Mix the chicken, roasted puréed vegetables, the broth mixture, the ground rice, and the fried garlic slices. Check for salt and add more fish sauce if needed. Heat the remaining chicken broth to boiling, remove from heat, and stir in the lime juice. Garnish *lap* with cilantro, scallions, and lime leaves. Serve with hot broth and salad leaves, herbs, and raw vegetables. *Serves 8*

Pumpkin Filled with Coconut Custard— A Traditional Festive Treat

1 small	pumpkin
6–8	eggs, depending on size of pumpkin
1–2 cans	coconut milk
1¼ C.	brown sugar
2 T.	rice flour, or cornstarch

Cut top from pumpkin—in an attractive star shape if possible—remove and discard seeds. Dry pumpkin inside with paper towels. Beat eggs until thick and light colored in a 4-cup measure. Pour coconut milk to equal the amount of eggs into a large bowl. Beat in eggs, sugar, and rice flour until thoroughly blended. Pour mixture into pumpkin shell, replace lid and steam, in a large steamer, for one hour, or until custard is set. Refrigerate until serving time. *Serves 6*

VIETNAM

Vietnamese food may well be the most healthful in Southeast Asia. Astonishing amounts of freshly picked leaves, herbs, vegetables, and roots are eaten at every meal, every day. Using only the leanest of meat, the Vietnamese cook with a minimal amount of oil, and turn up their noses at the lard used in the cooking of their Lao neighbors. Spicy Vietnamese dishes are a little less fiery than the chili-laced dishes of Thailand, though both countries favor fermented fish sauce, and identical varieties of chili peppers. Vietnamese food has a skillful blending of unusual flavors which creates a cuisine that is packed with flavor, yet with a delicacy of taste that is unique. China has had a decided influence on Vietnam's cooking, markedly so in the north, which is not surprising, since China dominated Vietnam for a thousand years. The Mongolian invasions, during the thirteenth century, generated a fondness for beef dishes, such as Mongolian Hot Pot. Chopsticks, bean curd, fermented soybeans, star anise, and rice noodles are all legacies of the Chinese, as is the uniquely Chinese technique of combining meat and shellfish in fillings and sausages. The Vietnamese have adapted all these foreign ideas to suit their own tastes, and in so doing have evolved a much lighter style of cooking that is uniquely their own. A different emphasis on the use of basic ingredients is apparent in the Vietnamese scant use of cooking oil and thickeners, such as cornstarch. The Chinese prefer cooked vegetables, the Vietnamese invariably eat them raw; shallots, rarely seen in a Chinese kitchen, are relied on heavily in Vietnamese cuisine as a base for cooked dishes as well as for garnishing; and soy sauce, ubiquitous as a flavoring in Chinese food, is scarcely to be found. The Vietnamese preference for *nuoc mam* (fermented fish sauce) is well known, and once having tasted their food, nobody could mistake it for Chinese. Favorite herbs in Vietnamese cooking are cilantro, basil, dill, and many kinds of fresh mint. Seasonings in daily use include chilies, garlic, shallots, lemongrass, ginger, galangal, shrimp paste, turmeric, tamarind, and lime juice.

Vietnam, the most easterly country on the Southeast Asian mainland, lies curved in an attenuated S-shape beside the South China Sea. From the Chinese border in the north to the Gulf of Thailand in the south, its coastline stretches 1,400 miles (2,253 kilometers). Vietnam's offshore territory encompasses many thousands of archipelagos, between the Gulf of Tonkin and the Gulf of Thailand. Deeply carved valleys, black gorges lit with waterfalls, and magnificent mountain ranges, create natural borders between Vietnam and her neighbors—China to the north, Laos to the west, and Cambodia to the south. The Annamite range extends from the Chinese border to Vietnam's Central Plateau. Despite the war's devastation, Vietnam is one of the most beautiful countries in the world, with lush jungles, glittering rice fields, and white powdery beaches. The Vietnamese often describe their country as shaped like a yoke with a rice basket suspended from each end. The rice baskets refer to the rice-growing Red River delta in the north and the Mekong delta in the south. Between the two rice baskets, the thin stretch of mountainous terrain, hugging the coast, forms the yoke, with the once royal city of Hue situ-

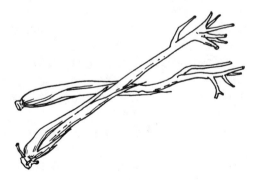

Lemongrass

Dill

ated midway between Hanoi and Saigon (Ho Chi Minh City). The
Red River flows from its source in China's Yunnan Province, across
Northern Vietnam to the South China Sea. The vast plains and valleys
of the fertile Red River delta, which includes the city of Hanoi, the
capital of the Socialist Republic of Vietnam, are home to nine-tenths
of the people living in northern Vietnam. The Red River delta saw the
beginnings of wet-rice farming by the Vietnamese in prehistoric times.
Now an elaborate 6,000-mile (9,656 kilometers) system of dikes pro-
tects the fields from yearly flooding which ruins the crops. Repairs are
constantly in progress to ward off calamity, as starvation strikes whenever a dike breaks. Saigon is the center for the immense southern rice
basket, irrigated by the Mekong—one of the longest rivers in the world.
Flowing across China from its source in Tibet, it forms the northern
border between Burma and Laos; crosses Laos, to carve the border

between Laos and Thailand; bisects Cambodia, and flows over the southern tip of Vietnam, molding the rich, fertile Mekong delta.

The land mass of the vast delta grows at a rate of 250 feet a year, as alluvial deposits build up on an immense shelf, lying just beneath the sea, at the mouth of the Mekong. The delta covers the area from the coast to the Cambodian border and all the way down to the southernmost part of Vietnam, which juts into the Gulf of Thailand. Endless rice fields stretch as far as the eye can see, interspersed with irrigation ditches and busy waterways transporting goods and people to and from Saigon.

Life in the delta revolves around water. Most of the food sold in markets arrives by boat, as do the shoppers carrying decorative, skillfully woven baskets. Slim, wooden boats, suited to the narrow waterways, are poled along by Vietnamese women wearing conical straw hats to protect them from the fierce sun. Only a few feet above sea level, monsoon rains inundate many of the provinces from July to October. The most productive agricultural area in the country, the delta provides not only enough rice to feed the people of the south and central area, but also some of the people in the north. More than half of the population of Vietnam live in the delta. They number around 3.5 million, making it one of the most densely populated parts of the world. In order to escape the overcrowded conditions, more and more people opt to live in houses on the water that are kept afloat by hollow metal drums. Metal fishing nets, suspended beneath the houses, trap fish, which are left in their natural habitat to be fattened up before being sent to market. This assures floating house owners both a living and living space. Approximately 62 million people live in Vietnam, and the population is still largely rural, despite the overcrowding in the cities of Hanoi and Saigon. About 80 percent are engaged in farming, fishing, and forestry, 20 percent in industry, commerce, and the military.

Roads, in passable condition, connect the nine provinces of the region. Most people living in low-lying areas earn their livelihood by growing rice and vegetables. In the Mekong delta the land is totally rural. Villages of stilt houses sit beside the canals. Their inhabitants labor from sunrise to sunset in the unending rice paddies. After the harvest, they spread the rice in long yellow bands along the sides of the roads to dry. Traditional Vietnamese culture is based on the settled lowland farmer's way of life rather than that of the nomadic highlanders. The Vietnamese are raised in large extended families, comprising three or more generations. Elderly members of the family are accorded great respect. Devotion to the family and village is paramount in rural society. The centuries-old values inherent in the agricultural way of life hold sway. Rural families work together, particularly those engaged in wet-rice farming. The entire year is spent tending the crop, and the efforts of the whole family, including women and children, are essential. The first task in the rice-growing cycle is preparation of the seed bed. The seedlings are cultivated in nurseries. When the delicate seedlings have grown enough to be moved, the rice paddies are plowed and flooded and the laborious, time-consuming transplanting can begin. The shoots have to be kept at just the right level of water, which is controlled by the dikes. Being able to control the water is paramount to a good harvest, and essential in areas where the rice paddies are terraced on mountainsides. Where there is a year-round supply from a river, water control enables the Vietnamese, and other rice-growing countries, to grow more than one crop a year. Harvesting is also strenuous, backbreaking work; though with the promise of a lavish harvest celebration on the immediate horizon, this is undertaken more joyously.

Rice is basic to the diet in Vietnam, as it is all over Southeast Asia. Many varieties are grown: differences are in texture, size of the grain, keeping qualities, color, and above all aroma and taste. The more fragrant and delicious the rice, the higher the price will be. Black and glutinous varieties are used mainly for desserts. Rice is bought

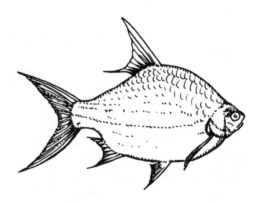

Cá he, raised in floating cages

from a rice dealer and it is essential to find a dealer who is both knowledgeable and trustworthy. Whenever possible, a Vietnamese prefers to buy his rice from a friend. Lately there have been complaints that the rice no longer has the same appetizing aroma or taste it once had. The Vietnamese government, in promoting the use of new strains of rice capable of producing more than one crop a year, has become the third largest exporter of rice in the world. However, the quality of rice for domestic consumption no longer compares favorably to the fragrant rice grown in Thailand. Rice is far and away the largest crop grown in Vietnam. Next are cassava (tapioca), coconuts, corn, cotton, sugarcane, and sweet potatoes. Some crops, such as tea, coffee, and rubber, are grown principally for exportation. Others, among them soy, sesame, peanuts, and castor beans, are grown to be processed into cooking oils for domestic use.

Saigon: Queen of the Mekong

The Mekong delta is dominated by Saigon (Ho Chi Minh City), the capital city of South Vietnam until reunification of the country in 1975. Cholon, Saigon's Chinatown, is the largest ethnic Chinese district in Vietnam. Cholon has been a thriving commercial area since 1778, when the first Chinese merchants came to Saigon. The Chinese-Vietnamese have always preferred urban dwelling. They live in their own neighborhoods, mainly in southern cities, often in very comfortable houses with exquisitely carved lintels around the doors and windows. Skilled in business affairs, with influential connections in other countries, they have long held significant positions in banking and commerce. Tightly packed shop houses with the traditional five-foot ways line the streets. Under these arcades, mobile food carts, stalls, and sidewalk vendors hawk their wares. Everything imaginable will be for sale on these chaotic, colorful streets. On the sidewalks, Indian fortune-tellers sit shuffling their cards, their caged "clairvoyant" bird beside them. The bird, let out of his coop, picks up one of the dealt cards, and hops over to its owner, who uses the card to predict the customer's future. Unsuccessful attempts by the government to assimilate the educated and resourceful Chinese-Vietnamese into mainstream society led to their persecution by the Communist government after reunification. Their businesses and property confiscated, Chinese-Vietnamese in the hundreds of thousands fled Vietnam, an economic and cultural loss Vietnam could ill afford.

Saigon is fast-paced and overcrowded, choked with buses, bicycles, pedicabs, and motor scooters. Vietnamese are energetic and hardworking. Young people flock to Saigon to try to make their way in the world, which contributes to the housing shortage and to the chronic problems the city has with electricity and plumbing. However, the easing of some restrictions is fostering private enterprise and with it hope for a brighter future. Saigon's huge Ben Thanh Market, thriving since its inception in 1914, covers an area of 7 square miles (11 square kilometers). Ben Thanh is a busy, lively place selling everything anyone could possibly need. Displays of brilliantly colored fruits and vegetables delight the eye. The back of the market is packed with food vendors, selling aromatic, local dishes and tempting snacks, such as rice-flour pancakes stuffed with prawns, bean sprouts, and onions; curries, spring rolls, succulent ears of corn boiled in their husks, sandwiches of pork pâté, and fragrant cups of filtered coffee, coconut juice, or freshly squeezed sugarcane juice. The distinctive smell of spices, indescribable dried ingredients, and pungent condiments blends with the perfume of ripening fruit and the fragrance of flowers. Smaller stalls, selling drinks, cigarettes, and various imported goods, crowd both the interior of the market and the surrounding streets. Ben Thanh is the place to find electric household appliances, as well as radios, cassette players, television sets, household items, and even clothing. Vietnamese women wear colorful, high-collared, long-sleeved tunics, slashed to the waist on the side seams, over a pair of white or black trousers. This form of dress is called *ao dai* and was introduced in the 1930s. In the 1700s, women were expected to wear long skirts. Also at that time, the fabric color and pattern worn by both sexes was dictated by professional status, social class, or ceremonial custom, that is, blue for official dress, yellow—a color for emperors only, and white for funerals. In the mid-1700s, long skirts were replaced by trousers in the central and southern parts of Vietnam. Buttons replaced sashes for jackets. Following the cessation of war in 1975, a ten-year period of austerity dictated a mandatory, uniform blouse and trousers for everyone. Happily, with the return of some of the traditional mores, the graceful *ao dai* is again in vogue.

Saigon's hundreds of restaurants reflect the cosmopolitan

makeup of the population, catering to Chinese, Indian, French, and American tastes. Cafés, reminiscent of Paris, sell coffee and patisserie; ice cream parlors echo their counterparts in the United States, and the good smells emanating from the curry restaurants are quintessentially Indian. In addition, as food is sometimes scarce, several government-run restaurants for the local people are open for lunch and dinner, serving precooked dishes at very reasonable prices.

A large percentage of the delta people are Khmer. They were among the first inhabitants of the delta region. From the ninth to the fifteenth century, the Khmer empire covered the entire area from the South China Sea to the Indian Ocean. Historical records indicate that the northern Red River delta had groups of nomadic tribes from southern China, as early as 3,000 B.C. These immigrants merged with Indonesian peoples already established there. For a thousand years the people of the Red River delta and China were at war with one another. Then as now, Vietnam was a vital link between India and China. The Vietnamese alternated brief periods of independence from Chinese overlords with longer periods of subjugation. The Vietnamese learned much from the Chinese, including use of the plow, the domestication of animals, dike buildings, and other irrigation techniques necessary for rice growing. In 938 A.D. the Vietnamese threw off the yoke of China and established the first Vietnamese Dynasty, the Ngo Dynasty. There were eleven dynasties in all—the last Emperor of Vietnam, Bao Dai, was ousted in 1955 by Ngo Dinh Diem.

Many other nations have influenced Vietnam history. Portuguese traders arrived in Vietnam in 1535, and introduced many new foods from the New World, among them potatoes and chili peppers. In 1600, French traders and Catholic missionaries established posts in Vietnam. The French launched their first major attack against Vietnam in 1847. In 1858 the French gained control, divided Vietnam into three separate colonial provinces, and ruled for almost one hundred years. Ousted by the Japanese during World War II, they returned after the war to an eight-year struggle against the Vietminh forces. The French were finally defeated at Dien Bien Phu in 1954. One year later, Bao Dai was deposed, after the country was divided into two nations by the Geneva Conference. Reunification occurred in 1975 after the Vietnamese War.

The French colonization of Vietnam has had a marked influence

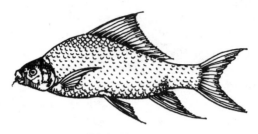

Cá ét (black carp)

on their tastes in food, spawning a love of café au lait, milk, yogurt, butter, ice cream, asparagus, white potatoes, pâté, and particularly, French bread and patisserie. An appreciation for French food is evident in the many Vietnamese-run French restaurants doing a thriving business in the major cities. Not surprisingly in light of their colonial past, Vietnamese restaurants in Paris greatly outnumber Chinese. This tendency is evident in other European capitals.

India introduced two great religions to Vietnam, Hinduism and Buddhism, and also their unique style of architecture. India's influence is found also in the fragrant, warm spices used to perfume curry—a dish that goes particularly well with rice.

Next to rice, the primary food for most of Southeast Asia is fish and shellfish from the South China Sea and from fresh inland waters. Mackerel, sardines, and tuna are caught in such quantities that some of the catch is frozen, or dried, and exported to neighboring countries. Tiny fishing villages along the coast depend on the bounty from the sea for their livelihood, as they have for hundreds of years. People not living near natural fishing grounds stock man-made ponds in their villages. There are as many methods of fishing, and types of fishing equipment, as there are different terrains in which to fish. Hilltribes use nets, poles and lines to combat the swiftly running mountain streams. Small round coracles, used to fish for squid, may be seen stacked on the beaches. These tiny flat-bottomed boats are taken out to sea in larger vessels. The actual fishing is done from the coracles at night, while the bright lights of the larger boat attract the squid to the surface. Tiny buttery-tasting fresh-caught squid are a great delicacy, especially when served with ginger and garlic sauce. Freshwater fishing is an industry in large river valleys and in the coastal estuaries. The abundant fish are either dried for export or made into fermented fish sauce, called *nuoc mam*. Beloved by the Vietnamese, this sauce replaces salt, which lacks *nuoc mam*'s nutritive qualities, and adds its distinctive taste to practically every dish. Some westerners find fish sauce too pungent for their palates, but judiciously used with other ingredients, its flavor is quite subtle. N*uoc mam* is made by layering anchovies and salt, and sometimes other fish, in wooden barrels and leaving it to ferment. After three months, the spigot is opened and liquid flows from the barrel, to be poured back over the anchovies and left fermenting for another three months until the first sauce—a clear, amber liquid—is syphoned off and bottled. There are several grades of fish sauce. The best, from the first draining, and made solely from anchovies, is expensive and well worth the cost. Lesser grades, used mostly in cooking, are made by adding water after the first extraction, and pressing out a second extraction. This grade is clearer, lighter in color, and less expensive. *Nuoc mam*, mixed with fresh chili, garlic, lime, and sugar, becomes *nuoc cham*, a dipping sauce used throughout Vietnam with most finger foods.

Fermented shrimp paste also seasons many foods throughout Southeast Asia. Available in jars in oriental markets, shrimp paste also comes in blocks. Shrimp paste needs to be toasted before adding to a dish. Fresh shrimp paste, called for in recipes such as shrimp fritters, is easily made by pounding fresh shrimp in a mortar, or mincing them briefly in a food processor. Other recipes using fresh shrimp paste are shrimp pâté, a mixture of fresh shrimp paste and minced aromatic vegetables bound with pork fat and eggs; and shrimp toast, which is served in all Asian restaurants on both sides of the Pacific Ocean. *Chao Tom*, grilled sugarcane wrapped in spiced fresh shrimp paste, is a very popular snack in Vietnam. Fresh shrimp balls add extra nutrition to fish broth, or chicken broth, spiked with *nuoc mam* and sliced scallions. Huge amounts of these delectable morsels are fried and consumed as snacks during the day, along with mounds of savory or sweet fritters—usually bought from street vendors. Fritters made from crab, fish, peanuts, potatoes, shrimp paste, ground pork and shrimp, assorted vegetables, and even minced frog meat, augment the evening meal. A specialty of the central region of Vietnam is a famous and substantial pancake, called Happy Pancake. Small spoonfuls of pork, shrimp, bean sprouts, mushrooms, garlic, and shallots are dropped onto a spoonful of pancake batter made fragrant with *nuoc mam*. Beaten egg is dribbled on top, the skillet is covered, and the pancake is lightly steamed. Folded in half like an omelette, and fried, the resulting treat is delightfully crisp and a deep golden brown. Vietnamese share the Chinese love of pork dishes. Poultry is also prevalent in Vietnamese dishes. Beef used to be too expensive to indulge in often, but lately, a government program to increase the number of cattle for beef consumption has had some success, and beef's appearance, at least on restaurants' menus, is more common.

Vietnam was a hunter's paradise for the French colonists. Diverse animal species in the forests and mountainous areas include rhinoceros, elephant, wild buffalo, tiger, panther, bear, monkey, crocodile, and tapir, among others. Vast tropical forests still cover two-fifths of Vietnam. But as forest products are used increasingly for export, forests are diminishing. Hard currency is badly needed in this desperately poor country. Hardwood timber, such as wood ebony and teak, is valued for making fine furniture and crafts; pine, oak, and bamboo for building houses. Oils, resin, medicinal plants, and various spices, including cinnamon and anise, are also worthwhile forest commodities. Many of the country's 60 minority groups—collectively referred to as Montagnards for their propensity for mountain dwelling—hunt, fish, and grow rice in cleared forest areas in the vicinity of their villages. They move from one cleared field to the next, as the soil is exhausted. They live in bamboo houses, usually raised above the ground on stilts. Music is very important to the Montagnards. They have different songs for different activities: hunting songs, fishing songs, marriage and love songs, ceremonial songs, and songs for sorcery. Gongs, usually made of bronze, are revered throughout Vietnam. Some tribes measure their wealth, not by the jewelry adorning their women, but by the number of gongs the tribe possesses.

Three regional cuisines distinguish the cooking of Vietnam: northern cuisine from the region centered on the fertile Red River delta and the city of Hanoi; central cuisine from Hue and the narrow, mountainous, ribbon along the coast; and southern cuisine from the immense low-lying alluvial plain of the Mekong delta and Saigon.

The cooking of northern Vietnam is considerably more bland than the cooking of the rest of the country. Since chili peppers do not grow in the colder climate of this region, dishes are flavored with black peppercorns and galangal—a weightier, somewhat translucent, pinkish variety of ginger. The emphasis is on stir-fries, rice soups, and cooked vegetables rather than raw. Soy sauce adds saltiness and color to food. Much less fish sauce is used than is common in the delta. Northern cooks make use of dark sesame oil, dried jellyfish, and dried fungi, such as wood-ear mushrooms, all beloved by the Chinese. The most popular fare in North Vietnam, and a specialty of the city of Hanoi, is *pho bo*. Essential to *pho bo* is a steaming hot, savory, beef stock, to be poured over rice noodles, thin strips of beef, bean sprouts, and herbs, just before serving. The ingredients barely cook and so retain their crisp freshness. P*ho* (pronounced far) is a specialty of foodstalls and street vendors. Stews, crab and asparagus soup, and a dish comprising well-seasoned stuffed bean curd, are also popular fare. A favorite winter dish, similar to Mongolian hot pot, is a pot of boiling broth over a charcoal stove, and everyone grouped around it with their chopsticks, immersing strips of meat and vegetables in the hot broth, until cooked to their satisfaction.

The Ancient Capital of Hanoi

Hanoi, the second-largest city in Vietnam and the oldest capital city in Southeast Asia, founded in A.D. 1010, is the seat of national government. Hanoi is situated in the bend of the Red River, and this is the origin of its name, from the Chinese characters Ha, meaning river, and Noi, meaning inside. Today there are 3 million inhabitants, and sometimes it seems as though almost as many bicycles clog the streets. Tree-lined boulevards and green and shady public parks, add charm to the city, as do the pagodas, temples, and many lakes. West Lake covers an area of 2,000 acres. Petit Lac is one of the most attractive. Also called the Lake of the Restored Sword, an old legend says this lake is inhabited by a golden turtle. Situated in the center of Hanoi, the park surrounding the Lake of the Restored Sword is popular in the early hours with young joggers, and also with the elderly who stand in groups doing stretching exercises in unison. Now that the restrictions against private enterprise have been lifted, booths have sprung up around the lake selling Vietnamese-made instant coffee, packets of tea, and various confections. A significant architectural legacy, left by the French colonists, has been badly damaged by years of war and neglect, but many ancient temples are being restored. Traditional architecture survives in the buildings in the Old Quarter that line alleys named Basket Street, Leather Street, Tin Street, and even Broiled Fish Street. In the Old Quarter, entrepre-nurial spirit is increasingly evident in the many new, privately owned restaurants and coffee shops.

Central cuisine revolves around Hue, which stands on the banks of the Perfume River. From 1802 to 1945, Hue was the imperial city of the Nguyen Dynasty. Palaces, citadels, and imperial mausoleums, many of them in excellent condition despite the bombing raids of 1968, still grace the city. Further south are the ruins of the Champa kingdom which was conquered and absorbed into Vietnam in 1306. The coastal strip at this point is so narrow that less than 50 miles of forested mountains separate Hue from the Lao border. Fishing is an important industry in this area, and the famous *nuoc mam* is produced here. In Hue, dishes are more sophisticated, and food presentation more elaborate and painstaking, as befits the elegant, former Royal capital of Vietnam. Known for the inventiveness of its cooks, spices are used copiously, along with their famed, aromatic fish sauce. A mixture of these two ingredients with tomato paste, stirred into soup, adds both color and exceptional flavor. French bread, purchased daily from the local bakeries, makes a splendid accompaniment to stir-fried or curried dishes. Food vendors sell wonderful, toasted sand-wiches from French bread, slathered with soft pork pâté, or piled with strips of spicy barbecued pork topped with salad vegetables, herbs, and a dollop of chili sauce. Crisp, yet moist, tiny rice cakes are another specialty of this region. Served with imaginative mixtures of pounded dried shrimp and chili pepper, or with pounded lemongrass and shallots, they make wonderfully satisfying snacks. Hue's famous pork sausages are particularly good. Sausage-making in Vietnam has bene-fitted from the expertise of both the French and the Chinese. Pâtés and boudins add elegance to Vietnamese meals, and may be bought at foodstalls inside the larger food markets. The Vietnamese have a sausage that is uniquely their own, called *Cha Lua*. Made from a finely ground mixture of pork, pork fat, and fresh shrimp, flavored with aromatic vegetables and pungent fish sauce, it is steamed for 20

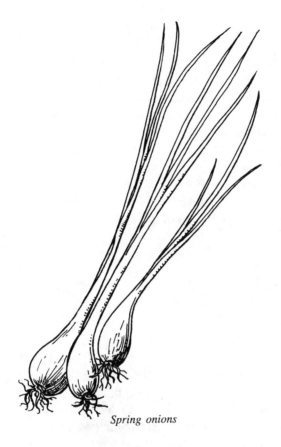

Spring onions

minutes to cook the pork completely, then fried to a rich brown color, and served with mint, coriander, salad greens, and *nuoc cham*. Central cuisine benefits from the many temperate fruits and vegetables that thrive in cooler climates. Among these are strawberry, plum, avocado, potato, artichoke, cauliflower, and asparagus. Tea plantations flourish in the dense forests. This hilly terrain is not conducive to the growing of wet rice. People living here partially support themselves by fishing the many rivers and streams. Closer to the coast, rivers draining from the highlands provide better conditions for wet rice farming, and the clear waters of the South China Sea provide a wealth of fresh fish, shellfish, and other delicacies.

Southern cooks make use of far more raw vegetables and herbs than cooks from the cooler north. Freshly picked green salad leaves, along with a sprig of herb, a sliver of scallion, a strip of cucumber, or a thin slice of pineapple, wrap delectable crispy spring rolls, called *cha gio*, served as the main meal in Vietnam rather than as an appetizer. The resulting bite-sized package is then dipped in *nuoc cham* before eating. Spring roll fillings differ with the whim of the cook, giving them an element of mystery. Recipes for these varied fillings include shrimp, pork, garlic, and scallions; beef, bean sprouts, onion, noodles, and crab meat; or pork, dried fungus, crab, mushroom, and egg. Barbecued meats and fish receive a similar leaf-wrapping treatment. The Vietnamese habit of wrapping foods in fresh greens and herbs encompasses not only finger foods—spring rolls, satay, and small sausages—but pieces of fish or meat taken, with the aid of chopsticks, from a stir-fried or curried dish. These morsels too will be wrapped and dunked in one of their zestful dipping sauces. *Nuoc leo*, an excellent, spicy hot sauce laced with lightly ground fresh peanuts, often accompanies meat and fish dishes. The fresh leaves, herbs, and sauces are a terrific combination; each bite is an explosion of flavor, and all of it healthful.

Many Buddhists are strict vegetarians, eating no animal products of any kind. All Buddhists are required for four days of the month to eat only vegetables: usually two days at the beginning of the month and two days in the middle. Meat, fish, eggs, and fish sauce are prohibited during these four days. Consequently, Vietnam has developed a vast repertoire of vegetarian recipes to fool the eye. These look-alike dishes use bean curd, coconut milk, fermented beans, dried and fresh mushrooms, to make foods that resemble meat, chicken, or fish. Vegetarian spring rolls are filled with well-shredded vegetables, such as potatoes, carrots, leeks, scallions, and bean sprouts, mixed with chopped bean curd and flavored with different varieties of dried fungus, to lend a meaty texture. They need to be very securely wrapped, as they are cooked longer than nonvegetarian spring rolls, and lack the moisture of meat or egg to bind the filling. The widespread use of legumes, nuts, and seeds, plus a profusion of fruit and vegetables accessible to the Vietnamese, is a boon for vegetarians. Rice is more plentiful in the south. The Mekong delta covers all of the southern part of Vietnam from south of the central highlands to the Gulf. Innumerable rivers and waterways, and also the long coastline, assure an astonishing variety and an ample supply of fresh fish throughout the year. Crustaceans such as sea urchins, abalone, and oysters are plucked from the sea and, as often as not, eaten on the spot. Exotic fruits and vegetables, sugarcane, and coconut plantations thrive in the humid heat.

The south is considerably wealthier than the north. Abundance characterizes the cooking of the south and cooks incline to sweeter and spicier dishes. Most salad dressings, dipping sauces, and virtually all cooked dishes contain the nutritious fish sauce, *nuoc mam*. Sugarcane and coconut contribute to the sweetness of the cooking, and an abundance of chili peppers to the increased heat. Raw fruit is often sliced and tossed into the cooking pot at the last minute.

Saigon has its own favorite soup, called *mee quang*, to rival the *pho bo* of Hanoi. Cucumber strips, lettuce leaves, bean sprouts, fresh herbs, and a handful of cooked rice noodles are put in individual soup bowls, which are then filled with a delectable hot broth, flavored with pork, chicken, fish sauce, and shrimp paste. Each bowl is garnished with crushed peanuts. Several restaurants specializing in beef, called Bo Bay Mon (Seven Beef Dishes), serve a seven-course meal, featuring a small amount of beef at each course, cooked in seven different ways. This famous meal is based on a traditional, special-occasion feast, common to the south. The first dish is a vinegar-flavored, beef fondue, and the last is a beef soup made from the fondue broth. Everybody cooks strips of paper-thin, raw beef in the boiling broth, piles the strips with vegetables and herbs, rolls them in a softened rice paper wrapper, and dunks the package in the *nuoc cham*. Much of the actual cooking is done at the table, with guests participating in the final stages of preparation. The Vietnamese are happy to stay up late, and streets are lively well into the night. People frequent the many restaurants and foodstalls selling crispy, rice paper wrapped, spring rolls, roasted rice flour crackers encrusted with sesame seeds, and lemongrass flavored satays with peanut sauce. Immensely popular is *cha ca*, barbecued fish, and various minced fish cakes and stir-fried beef dishes.

The Vietnamese are an energetic and enterprising people. At least 95 percent literate, they are skilled artisans and craftsmen making both decorative and practical products. Their intricately patterned, handwoven baskets have many uses. Huge, handsome ones overflow with produce in the marketplace, round flat woven trays winnow grain, and individual lidded baskets, filled with hot rice, grace tables at mealtimes.

Vietnam's Myriad Religions

Vietnam's religious beliefs differ markedly from those of their neighbors. Though Buddhism is the religion of the majority of Vietnamese, their social structure is based on Confucianism, and Taoism permeates their still fervent animistic beliefs. Confucianism, based on the teaching of a sixth-century Chinese scholar, is very much concerned with education and learning. More a code of ethics than a religion, Confucianism was taught in Vietnamese schools. Taoist influence is through magic. Powerful Taoist priests play an authoritative role in village religious rituals and festivals using astrology and other means. Approximately two million Vietnamese are Roman Catholic or Protestant, and another million or so follow the Hoa Hao faith—a derivation of Buddhism. Catholic priests, and Buddhist monks and nuns, strong advocates of social and political change, have long provided medical assistance for the Vietnamese people, founding hospitals throughout the country. After reunification, most missions and churches were closed, causing the exodus of many Roman Catholics. Under Communist rule, organized religion has not fared well. Ancestor worship still thrives. People believe the spirits of their ancestors have the power to help them and protect them from harm.

The most important holiday in Vietnam is *Tet*. The whole country explodes with revelry during this celebration. New Year starts, usually in January or February, with a week-long bonanza, ending with a fabulous feast of costly delicacies. These are especially prepared to welcome home the spirits of the ancestors. The family altar is piled with fruits and special foods. Glutinous rice cakes are a traditional symbol of *Tet*. In Hanoi, they are filled with highly spiced pork, wrapped in banana leaves and steamed; in Hue and Saigon, the same glutinous rice cakes are preferred sweetened with bananas and coconut meat. *Tet* would not be *Tet* without rice cakes. No cooking is allowed during this festival. The special dishes are all prepared ahead of time, from recipes with the longest keeping qualities, and lots of spices to preserve the food. Candies are much in evidence. *Tet* is a time for new beginnings. The first week and particularly the first day of the New Year is of great importance, symbolizing one's good fortune for the rest of the year. Family reunions, the mending of old quarrels, payment of debts, new clothes, and feasting are the order of the day. Homes are scoured in preparation for the holiday, and decorated with peach blossoms, a symbol of peace and good fortune. At midnight on the last day of the old year, gongs, drums, and firecrackers herald the New Year.

Vietnamese do not categorize foods as suitable for breakfast, lunch, or dinner. They eat whatever they want or need at each meal—generally consuming quite a bit more early in the day. For family meals, generally three or four dishes will be served: steaming hot rice, a stir-fried dish, a main dish, such as curry or another well-sauced dish, and a soup. Rice bowls, a small plate, chopsticks, and a spoon are set at each place. As a sign of respect, children ask permission to eat from elder members of the family. Once each family member has put a little rice in their bowl, chopsticks are used to pick up a small amount of food from one dish, placing it on top of the rice. The bowl is then lifted to almost chin height before eating. Trying to convey food using chopsticks from a bowl placed on the table to your mouth is considered bizarre. When not in use, chopsticks are placed side by side across the rice bowl. It is considered unlucky to leave them in the food. Mixing food from several dishes together with your rice is socially inept. Soup may be sipped throughout the meal, or served at the end. Fresh fruit is almost always the preferred finale to the meal. Sometimes, if it is a special occasion, or if guests are present, a dessert, such as bananas and tapioca pudding steamed in banana leaves, bean curd custard, or steamed coconut pudding, might be prepared.

Guests are served tea, or other drinks, with an appetizer or two, before being escorted to the table. Tea drinking is an important ritual to the Vietnamese. It would be unthinkable not to offer tea at once to any visitor. A large pot of tea, enough to last the day, is prepared in the morning. A little of this strong tea is diluted with hot water. The many tea varieties belong to two basic types: green tea, which is made from leaves roasted immediately upon harvesting, and black tea, made from leaves left to ferment before roasting. Floral teas—

lotus, jasmine, chrysanthemum, and other flowers—contain whole dried blossoms which unfold in the hot water. Vietnam produces over fifty varieties of wine, mostly from rice. A strong alcoholic drink, served warmed for very special occasions, is brewed from black glutinous rice. Most beer is imported, and surprisingly inexpensive, as is vodka and Eastern European brandy. Street vendors everywhere sell soft drinks, fruit juices, and slightly sweetened coconut milk.

When planning your menu, try to have dishes with contrasting flavors and textures—a sweeter dish with a bitter or salty one, crunchy roasted peanuts with soft boiled noodles. Usually, the more delicately flavored dishes are served first, ending with the more assertive. The equipment found in a Western kitchen is more than adequate for cooking Vietnamese dishes. Having said that, there are one or two things that could make life a bit easier. These are an electric coffee grinder for pulverizing dried spices, and a mini food processor for making pastes from small quantities of fresh ingredients. Small skillets and small pans are invaluable for toasting seeds, spices, chilies, and nuts, and for cooking small amounts of sauce. Sharp knives for slicing meat, poultry, and fish, and swivel peelers for both peeling and cutting strips from vegetables are a must. A steamer, either from a well-stocked Asian market or from a Western one, is also a useful item to have for cooking Vietnamese foods.

Recipes from Vietnam

Beef Soup (Pho bo)

Broth

8	C.	beef broth
4		slices of ginger, about 1 inch across
1		inner stalk of lemongrass
4	large	shallots, thinly sliced
½		cinnamon stick
2	T.	fish sauce
12	oz.	beef steak
½	lb.	rice sticks, soaked 20 minutes in warm water and drained
1	T.	peanut oil

Garnishes

2		red chilies, seeded and sliced (use rubber gloves)
¼	lb.	bean sprouts, trimmed
½	C.	mint leaves
½	C.	cilantro leaves
½	C.	young spinach leaves, cut in thin strips
I		lime cut in quarters
3	T.	chili paste with garlic
3	t.	hoisin sauce

Simmer beef broth, ginger, lemongrass, 3 shallots, and cinnamon stick for one hour. Strain and discard solids. Mix in fish sauce and set aside.

Partially freeze steak, then slice paper thin. Toss with remaining shallot and refrigerate until 30 minutes before ready to use. Arrange sliced chilies, bean sprouts, mint, cilantro, spinach, and lime quarters attractively on a platter. Put chili paste and hoisin sauce into two tiny serving bowls. Heat to a rolling boil about 3 quarts of water in a large saucepan, and add peanut oil. Drop rice sticks into boiling water, and as soon as water returns to the boil, drain, and place in a heated bowl. Separate them with a fork. Heat broth to boiling. Divide beef and shallots among four deep, warmed soup bowls. Pour on boiling stock (beef will be cooked in seconds). Divide rice sticks among the four bowls and serve immediately. Each person then mixes vegetable garnishes and sauces into their soup.   *Serves 4*

Catfish and Noodle Soup

4	T.	fish sauce
1–2	t.	finely shredded fresh ginger
I	t.	sea salt
½	t.	black pepper
¾	lb.	catfish fillets
2	oz.	rice sticks, soaked in water for 20 minutes
2	T.	peanut oil
½	t.	Madras curry powder
2	t.	finely minced, tender lemongrass
I		medium-sized onion, thinly sliced
1½	t.	shrimp paste
I	t.	turmeric

5 C.	simmering water
1	lime, cut into wedges
3 T.	whole cilantro leaves

In a medium bowl, mix 2 tablespoons of fish sauce with the ginger, salt, and pepper. Slice the catfish into bite-sized pieces and stir into the fish sauce mixture, coating the catfish with sauce. Set aside to marinate. In a large heavy-bottomed pan, heat the oil over medium heat and stir-fry the curry powder, lemongrass, onion, and shrimp paste for 6 or 7 minutes, or until onion has softened, breaking up the shrimp paste against the side of the pan. Stir in the turmeric until well mixed, then add the simmering water, the rice sticks, and the remaining fish sauce. Bring to the boil, reduce heat, and simmer for 5 minutes. Stir in the catfish, again bring to the boil, reduce heat, and simmer gently until the fish is opaque—about 3 or 4 minutes. Pour into heated bowls, divide the cilantro leaves among the bowls, and serve with lime wedges.   *Serves 4–6*

Shrimp Toast

8	slices of day-old bread
	peanut oil for frying toasts
	lettuce or arugula leaves
	scallions
	mint leaves
	Vietnamese coriander sprigs

For shrimp paste

10 oz.	shrimp, peeled and deveined
2 T.	minced pork fat, or butter
1 T.	fish sauce
2 t.	peanut oil
½ t.	sea salt
	freshly ground pepper, to taste
1	egg white

Whirl all ingredients in a food processor to a soft paste—do not over-process. Or pound shrimp and pork fat or butter to a paste in a mortar and pestle, and mix with remaining ingredients.

Remove crusts, and slice bread in half lengthwise. Spread each piece with 2 to 3 tablespoons of shrimp paste. Pour enough oil into large skillet to generously coat bottom, heat to simmering, and place toasts in pan, shrimp side down. Fry, turning once, until golden brown, adding a little more oil if necessary. Serve hot with vegetables and herbs for garnishing, and *nuoc cham* sauce for dipping.

Makes 16 toasts

Nuoc Cham *sauce*

I	garlic clove, peeled
I	fresh hot red pepper, seeds removed
2 t.	sugar
½	fresh lime
2 T.	Vietnamese fish sauce
2 T.	water, or to taste

Using a food processor or a mortar and pestle, make a paste with the garlic, chili pepper, and sugar. Squeeze in lime juice, add lime pulp, fish sauce, and water. Mix well, adding more water, a few drops at a time, if the sauce is too strong.

Stir-fried Chicken Strips

10 oz.	chicken breast, cut in strips
2 T.	fish sauce
¼ t.	freshly ground black pepper
I	garlic clove, minced
2 T.	peanut oil
I	hot red chili, seeded and sliced
¼ lb.	mushrooms, sliced
2	scallions, sliced
2 T.	tomato sauce or I fresh tomato, peeled, seeded, and diced
¼ lb.	snow peas, trimmed

Toss chicken with fish sauce, black pepper, and garlic. Heat oil in a wok until shimmering, rapidly stir-fry chicken strips until opaque, remove from wok with a slotted spoon, and keep warm. Stir-fry red chili, mushrooms, and scallions for 3 or 4 minutes over high heat. Stir in tomato sauce or diced tomato, and return chicken and any juices to wok. Stir to heat evenly. Toss in snow peas for 20 to 30 seconds. Serve immediately.   *Serves 2–3*

Spring Rolls with Dipping Sauce

1	oz.	transparent rice noodles
½	C.	fresh shrimp, chopped
½	C.	crabmeat
½	C.	minced pork
½	small	onion
3		shallots
1		garlic clove
½	small	dried red pepper, seeds removed
¼	t.	sea salt
1	t.	sugar
1	T.	fish sauce
½	C.	fresh bean sprouts, trimmed and halved
½	t.	freshly ground black pepper
1		egg beaten
1		package round rice papers
		vegetable oil for frying

In a small bowl, place the noodles to soak for 20 minutes in warm water. Drain and cut into 1-inch pieces. Soak chili pepper in warm water for 10 minutes and drain. Place the cellophane noodles, shrimp, crabmeat, and pork in a mixing bowl. In a food processor, mince the red pepper, onion, shallots, and garlic, and add to the bowl. Stir in sea salt, fish sauce, black pepper, and bean sprouts. Mix thoroughly with shrimp mixture.

Place several rice paper wrappers on a flat surface. Using a pastry brush, coat one wrapper with beaten egg. It will soften in a few seconds. Place 2–3 tablespoons of filling one-fourth of the way in from the edge of the wrapper closest to you. Shape filling into a rectangle about 5 inches long and ¾-inch wide. Fold the lower edge of the wrapper over the filling and roll up, folding in the sides of the wrapper after the second turn. Repeat until all the filling is used.

Pour vegetable oil into an electric frying pan to a depth of 3 inches. Heat oil to 350°, slide spring rolls into the oil, and cook uncovered until golden brown. Remove spring rolls to paper towel to drain. Serve at once with *nuoc cham* sauce (see recipe page 99).

Grilled Beef with Lettuce, Herbs, and Nuoc Cham

1 lb.	flank steak strips
1	thin, hot red chili pepper, sliced
1 slice	red onion, chopped
2 T.	lemongrass, chopped
3	garlic cloves, chopped
1 T.	dark sesame oil
¼ t.	freshly ground black pepper
1 strip	lime zest, minced
2 T.	lime juice
2 T.	fish sauce
1 T.	water
1	head of red leaf lettuce, washed and dried, for wrapping
⅓ C.	unsalted peanuts, toasted and chopped
	mint leaves
	Vietnamese coriander or cilantro sprigs
4	scallions, sliced in 3-inch strips

Lightly freeze beef, then slice into very thin strips. Set aside. Place bamboo skewers in water to soak (this prevents conflagration later). In a food processor, blend the chili, onion, lemongrass, garlic, sesame oil, pepper, zest, lime juice, fish sauce, and water to a paste. Toss beef with chili paste, and refrigerate for at least 6 hours. Meanwhile, make *nuoc cham* sauce and refrigerate.

When ready to cook, scrape most of the marinade from beef strips and thread beef on bamboo skewers. Preheat charcoal grill or broiler, cook for 2 minutes, turn and cook 1 minute more—for medium raw. Serve beef surrounded with bowls of lettuce, peanuts, and herbs. Roll beef with a sprig of herbs, a strip of scallion, and a sprinkling of peanuts in a lettuce leaf and dunk in *nuoc cham* (see recipe page 99).

Serves 4

Vietnamese Stir-fried Pork with Rice Sticks

6 oz.	rice sticks
2 T.	peanut oil
1 lb.	pork tenderloin, thinly sliced
2 C.	chopped onion

1		minced garlic clove
		1-inch wide slice of fresh ginger, minced
2	T.	fish sauce
¼–½	T.	freshly ground black pepper
1½	C.	lightly steamed spinach, drained
⅓	C.	sesame seeds, toasted
2	T.	sliced scallions

Soak rice sticks in warm water for 20 minutes. Drain. Bring a large saucepan of water to a rolling boil, drop rice sticks in boiling water for 30 seconds, drain again and keep warm. Heat 1 tablespoon of oil in a wok over high heat, stir-fry pork until browned and cooked through. Remove from wok, set aside in a warm place. Stir-fry onions, garlic, and ginger until lightly browned, return meat to pan, add fish sauce and pepper, and stir-fry for 2 minutes more.

To serve, divide rice sticks among four warmed bowls and toss with a little *nuoc cham* sauce (see recipe page 99). Divide spinach and meat mixture and place on top of noodles. Sprinkle with sesame seeds and chopped scallions. Pass remaining *nuoc cham* sauce separately.

Serves 4

Bean Curd with Vegetables and Noodles in Coconut Milk

2	oz.	cellophane noodles
3–4		tender carrots, julienned
1	C.	cauliflower florets
1	lb.	firm bean curd
½	C.	peanut oil
4		shallots, minced
2		thin slices of ginger
1	C.	coconut milk
2	T.	Tamari sauce or soy sauce
1	t.	sea salt
½	t.	sugar
1	small	garlic clove, finely minced
		fresh coriander leaves, for garnish

Soak cellophane noodles in 1 quart of warm water for 20 minutes, drain, and set aside. Meanwhile, blanch carrots and cauliflower florets for 1 minute in boiling water. Drain, reserving ¼ C. water, and set aside. Pat dry the bean curd with paper towels and cut into 1-inch cubes. Heat oil in a wok over high heat and fry bean cubes until golden brown. Drain on paper towel, and keep warm. Pour off most of the oil, leaving about 1 tablespoon, and, over medium heat, stir-fry the shallots and ginger for 1 minute. Stir in carrots and cauliflower, and cook for 30 seconds. Add bean curd and coconut milk, Tamari or soy sauce, salt, sugar, garlic, and reserved water. Bring gently to the simmer, add cellophane noodles, lower heat, partially cover, and simmer for 5 minutes. Serve immediately, garnished with whole coriander leaves.

Serves 3–4

Banana Nut Cake

¾	C.	flour
1	t.	baking powder
1½	lb.	heavy, ripe bananas (about five)
2		eggs
½	C.	brown sugar
⅓	C.	cream
1	t.	vanilla extract
½	C.	coarsely chopped cashews
½	C.	freshly grated coconut

Preheat oven to 325°F. Sift flour with baking powder, set aside. Peel bananas, cut each one in four, and crush with the tines of a fork or a flat knife. Do not mash. Beat eggs and sugar with an electric mixer or in the processor until pale and thick. Pour into a bowl and using a wooden spoon, stir in cream, then flour. Do not overbeat. Add vanilla. Fold in bananas, cashews, and coconut and pour batter into a 9-inch greased cake pan. Bake for 45 minutes or until tester comes out clean. Turn onto a rack to cool.

Serves 8

MALAYSIA
AND SINGAPORE

Malaysians like their food to be enriched with coconut milk and generously spiced with chili peppers. Scorchingly hot *sambals* are served with meals for dunking finger foods. Seafood, chicken, and meats are prepared in countless ways, but a method universally esteemed, either for a meal or for a quick snack, is barbecued *satay*. In every town and village, food vendors, carrying a small charcoal brazier slung from a bamboo pole, will set down their grill on demand, and barbecue a skewer loaded with morsels of chicken, shrimp, pork, or goat meat. *Satay ayam* (chicken) is usually accompanied by a sweet dipping sauce made with fish sauce, spices, and crushed peanuts; *satay udang* (shrimp) has a tart, spicy lime or tamarind sauce. Steamed rice cakes, traditionally wrapped in palm leaves, are served with this succulent barbecue. Curries, immensely popular, are all based on a finely ground spice paste called *rempah*. *Rempah* is gently cooked in hot oil to release its fragrance, before adding the meat, fish, or vegetables.

Malaysia is a melting pot, and its eclectic cuisine reflects this broad racial mix. Malaysian cooking has undergone several transformations, assimilating the foods and cooking techniques of its many foreign settlers. The Arabs were among the first to come, bringing onions, almonds, pistachios, raisins, and kebabs—the original *satays*. Next came Indians adding to Malaysian cuisine their great breads, rice pilaus, curry spices, and unique vegetarian dishes. Indonesians brought fierce chilies, and the Chinese soy sauce, noodles, bean sprouts, and the wok. Regional differences in Malaysia's cuisine are also apparent. Northern Malaysians prefer the sour flavors of citrus and tamarind pulp to the sweeter, coconut-loaded cooking of the south. Eating places are equally diverse: Chinese noodle shops, Indian bread shops, Malay and Thai restaurants, American fast-food kiosks, markets selling farm-fresh, prepared foods, and hundreds of street vendors and foodstalls. Food vendors spring into action on the streets of every town and village after dark. Some of them specialize in only one dish. The quality of the food produced with such speed by the street vendors is extremely high, and for those who want authentic Malaysian dishes, the foodstalls are the place to find them. *Laksa Lemak*, a spicy noodle soup with seafood, *Soto Ayam*, spicy chicken soup; *gado gado*, a vegetable salad with spicy peanut sauce eaten throughout Southeast Asia; *Tahu goreng*, fried bean curd with a vegetable melange, flavored with crunchy peanuts or soy sauce; *Sambal Belacan*, a pungent chili dipping sauce; and *gula melaka*, a sweet dessert of sago and coconut milk which takes its name from Malaccan palm sugar, are all foodstall specialties. Sweet tastes are as prevalent in Malaysia as spicy. In fact, Malaysians have a passion for sweet desserts that is totally unlike other Southeast Asian countries, where, customarily, meals end with fresh fruit. Desserts make liberal use of sago, coconut, mung beans, palm sugar, and sticky rice, generally flavored with clove, cardamom, cinnamon, or nutmeg. Pandanus leaf

is as ubiquitous in Asian desserts as vanilla is in Western ones. Coconut milk is essential to Malaysian cooking. Chilled, it is also a popular drink on a steamy, tropical day.

The earliest inhabitants of Malaysia came from China's Yunnan Province: the first wave around 2500 B.C. and the second wave in 300 B.C. Later, people from Indonesia crossed the Straits and settled on the peninsula. The Malaysian language is almost identical to Indonesian. The two countries share many customs and their cuisines are also very much alike. Lured by tales of the wealth of Malacca, the Menangkabau tribes from West Sumatra crossed the water and settled in the hills behind the city. Here they founded their own principalities, governed by their own laws, and continued their matrilineal social system, where inheritance is through the female line. They also brought to Malaysia their distinctive and charming style of architecture. The Menangkabau revere the buffalo, and build the roofs of their houses in two swooping hornlike peaks. Many are crowned with multiple peaks, as are several of their state government buildings in Seramban. Traces of Malacca's early history are still to be found in the crumbling Portuguese fort, the Dutch church in the town's center, and the old well—the single source of pure water that saved the life of the city through several sieges.

The peninsula of West Malaysia stretches southward from the Thai border to the Straits of Malacca, narrowly skirting the Indonesian island of Sumatra. Singapore, formerly part of the Federation of Malaysia, lies at the southern tip of the peninsula. East Malaysia, separated from West Malaysia by 400 miles of the South China Sea, encompasses the states of Sabah and Sarawak on the northern coast of the island of Borneo. Though Sabah and Sarawak make up 60 percent of the land mass of Malaysia, 86 percent of the population live on the peninsula. The capital, Kuala Lumpur, the major industries and plantations, and the political power of Malaysia, are also on peninsular Malaysia. The exportation of tin, pepper, petroleum, palm oil, and rubber, Malaysia's impressive natural resources, has improved her standard of living. Rubber originally grew wild only in Brazil. Plantations on Java, Sumatra, and Borneo thrive today through the efforts of an enterprising British botanist who smuggled seeds from Brazil in the 1800s, had them germinated in Kew Gardens, and transplanted them to Southeast Asia.

Malays, Chinese, Indians, and many indigenous tribal groups make up the population of Malaysia. The country is officially Muslim, and all Malays follow Islamic law. The Indians are primarily Hindu, the Chinese mostly Buddhist and Christian, and the several indigenous tribal groups are mainly animists or spirit worshipers. The inhabitants of East Malaysia are also Christian, converted by missionaries who came to help develop the region. All refer to themselves as Malaysians.

The seas around the Malay and Indonesian archipelagos were once travel lanes for traders and explorers, questing for the fortunes to be made from spices. The town of Malacca, on the west coast, became the center for trading in no less than 84 different languages. Arab traders brought Islam to Malacca, converting all Malays to this faith by the second half of the fifteenth century. Easily defensible on a navigable river, the port of Malacca grew quickly, and was soon the richest seaport in the world. Piracy was rampant. Unfortunately, Malacca fell from power almost as quickly as it rose. The Portuguese subjugated Malacca in 1511. The Dutch ousted the Portuguese a hundred years later. In 1785, the British settled on the Island of Penang and eventually colonized the whole of Malaysia. Singapore became a jewel in the British crown. Western Malaysia won its independence from Britain in 1957, Eastern Malaysia in 1963. Today the Malacca River looks as though it has survived the intervening centuries unchanged. Ancient junks, with high poop decks, still cluster at dockside, looking for all the world like the junks that brought the first Chinese traders to Malaysia. The Chinese are the largest minority in the country. Traders since the thirteenth century in the Indonesian and Malayan archipelago, they came in large numbers in the nineteenth century, fleeing floods, famine, and political unrest. Preferring city living, the Chinese tend to stick to their own mores. They are proud to be able to trace their lineage in Malaysia back several centuries. Malacca's ancient Chinese section continues to be inhabited by descendants of immigrants who came to Malacca during the Ming Dynasty. Their quaint row houses have red tiled roofs that overhang the balconies, and shade the brightly lacquered shutters and doors. The Cheng Hoon temple, or Temple of Bright Clouds, founded in 1645, is the oldest in Malaysia. Mythical figures, birds, and flowers, fashioned from gleaming porcelain and glass, adorn the façade. Chinese Buddhist temples here are different from those in other Southeast Asian countries—not all of them are dedicated to Buddha. Many honor Kuan Yin, the Goddess of Mercy. Traditional Chinese funeral rituals have not changed. They still last at least a week. The family stay secluded, occupying themselves in making piles of paper money, paper cars, and elaborate paper houses, complete with gardens, servants, household pets, television, and video sets— all to be burned at the funeral for the deceased's use in the afterlife, along with his or her personal effects. The Chinese, whose work ethic is inherent in their three main religions—Buddhism, Confucianism, and Taoism—have enjoyed considerable success in economic affairs. Muslim Malays feel they are being financially eclipsed by the Chinese. Recently new laws have been enacted which, among other things, favor Malays in elections, in business affairs, and in the number of places available to them in universities. This has caused a certain amount of racial discontent.

Indians account for less than 10 percent of the population. They too came first as traders to the Straits of Malacca. But not until the British needed laborers for tin mining and rubber plantations did they come to stay, and in large numbers. A highly visible people in their brightly colored clothes, they are given to elaborate and equally colorful religious festivals that can last for days. Their Hindu religion manifests itself in many dazzling temples, every inch of their façades decorated with statues of Indian deities, gilded chariots, and sacred cows, all festooned with tinsel. Indians too are city dwellers.

Kuala Lumpur: Mosques, Minarets, and Princely Palaces

Many Malaysian towns were originally trading posts, established by the Dutch, the Portuguese, and the British. British towns were always built around a central green, called a *padang*, used for parades and all ceremonial occasions, although its major use was undoubtedly as a cricket pitch. Other towns, such as Johore, were originally capital cities within the empire of a Sultan. A rash of new towns, among these Kuala Lumpur, were started by the tin rush. These towns were usually badly run, filthy, and disease-ridden with wooden huts, bars, and shops sprawling in all directions. When Frank Swettenham, the British resident of Selangor, took over Kuala Lumpur in the late 1800s, the town was little more than a cluster of shacks in the encroaching jungle. His administration widened the streets, and rebuilt the town using brick and stone. The British Selangor Club was built along one side of the central green and a railway line was inaugurated in 1886. Eventually KL, as it is affectionately called, was on its way to becoming the colonial capital. In 1946, the headquarters of the Federation of Malaya set up here. The architecture of many of the buildings, such as the Supreme Court and the railroad station, have decidedly Moorish features—dome-topped towers and graceful arches, flood-lit at night. Minarets salute Islam; the slim tower of the National Mosque, the spiritual center of KL, rises above the skyline; and colonial architecture survives among the gleaming skyscrapers and modern office blocks. The National Palace, the King's official residence, is in the northern part of the city. A crown, surmounting the golden dome, heralds its royal status. Oddly, the monarch in democratic Malaysia is changed automatically every five years as each of the nine hereditary sultans takes a turn at being king. Most Sultans have their own personal palace in Kuala Lumpur, and the National Palace is relegated to Royal garden parties and other ceremonial occasions.

Malaysians, warm and easygoing, share a love of fun and good times. Everyone turns out to enjoy the many splendid feast days in the calendars of the seven or eight major religions in Kuala Lumpur. Races, games, contests, and parades are eagerly attended. Top spinning is a national pastime. Malaysians are proud of their brightly colored tops, which may be simply or ornately decorated, heavy or light, and of any size. In many villages, top spinning involves serious competition as participants vie to keep their top spinning longer than anyone else. Spinning times of well over an hour have been recorded. The game engenders great enthusiasm among the spectators, and bets on the outcome are often taken. Theatrical performances, depicting magical legends, are much-loved by Malaysians, as are renditions calling for loud and enthusiastic percussionists, thumping instruments fashioned from coconuts to hollowed out logs. Some malls arrange these performances to entertain people as they shop.

Vendors on the streets of KL, and in marketplaces, cater to the food preferences of the different races, offering *satays*, Chinese noodle dishes, delicious hot Indian breads, and Indian banana leaf curries. After six o'clock, along the riverbank in KL, foodstalls fire up their charcoal braziers, and with astonishing speed, turn out all manner of spicy dishes and snacks, usually washed down with glasses of sugarcane juice. Fruit juice and sugarcane juice are Malaysia's preferred thirst quenchers. The juices are freshly made with interesting blends of different juices, particularly in southern Malaysia, where they are served with a splash of sugar syrup. Curiously, closer to the Thai border in the north, juice is routinely served with a sprinkling of salt. Ice *kacang* is a drink and dessert in one, made with beans, corn kernels, and coconut milk laced with red syrup and poured over ice. Muslims are forbidden to drink alcohol. Hard liquor is extremely expensive to buy—beer is somewhat cheaper. Chinese Malaysians have no such prohibitions and alcohol is easy to find in Chinatown. It is also freely available in hotels.

The famous Malay Sunday Market—which runs from Saturday night until the wee hours of Sunday morning—sells jewelry, crafts, pottery, silverware, embroidery, batik, and all kinds of handicrafts. Malay dishes are sold at foodstalls and restaurants within the market. The racial mix in KL is fascinating. Strolling the aisles will be Chinese in loose pajama outfits, Indians in dhotis or Nehru jackets, Malaysian women in colorful sarongs, and Muslim women wearing their traditional head coverings. Nowadays, blue jeans, T-shirts, and Western-style business suits are also common. Dress, and Islam's extensive food taboos, set Malays apart. Pork is forbidden to Muslims, and many prefer to eat *halal* food that conforms to their religious tenets. This food is prepared only by Muslims. Intermarriage is rare. Due to Malaysia's older matrilineal societies, women have far greater autonomy and more freedom than Muslim women in many other regions of the world. Here women own property, manage their own businesses and finances, and often make key family decisions.

Chinatown lies close to the river in the older part of Kuala Lumpur. Arcades, built in front of the Chinese two-story shophouses called the "five-foot ways," shade the street. The whole area is one vast thriving bazaar selling everything and anything—from crocodile shoes to crocodile steaks. Under the arcades, fortune tellers predict the future, and snake charmers entertain the throng. Shops and restaurants open onto the five-foot ways. Food orders are taken in the doorways and inside Chinese cooks can be seen concocting dishes to tempt the appetite. Indian cooks serve fragrant *naan* and *chapati* in front of their shops. On street corners Chinese medicinal potions, guaranteed to cure whatever ails you, sell briskly. Once the sun goes down, the shops close and a thriving night market springs to life, selling all the elegant counterfeit designer goods imaginable. The Central Market, which was once a major produce market stocked by the surrounding farmers, has become a splendid art-deco building, its lofty ceilings painted blue and pink; it now houses the Handicraft Center. Here shoppers are entertained with live performances of shadow puppets or song and dance shows while browsing. All manner of well-made and generally reasonably priced crafts are for sale. In the heart of Chinatown is the Chow Kit market, reputed to have the best and cheapest food in all of Kuala Lumpur. Sunday morning crowds throng the market, noisily haggling over inexpensive household goods, fresh produce, and snacks to augment the evening meal.

A typical family meal would have a meat or fish dish, one or two vegetables dishes, and a soup. These dishes are served at room temperature, and eaten with the fingers of the right hand—never the left. Hundreds of Malaysians are convinced fingers taste better than forks. But nowadays forks and spoons are put at each place setting. Steamed rice (*nasi*) is the staple food in all three cuisines—Malay, Chinese, and Indian. Each cuisine uses the same basic ingredients. The preparation differs somewhat, and religious differences play an important role in the choice of meats. Malays abhor pork in any form, some Indians eschew beef, while many are strict vegetarians. An important ingredient in vegetarian cooking is tempe, fermented bean curd pressed into cakes. Chinese cuisine would suffer greatly without pork. It is far and away their favorite meat, and is essential to many of their delectable dishes. Noodles too play a large part in Chinese cuisine. Their popularity has spread throughout Southeast Asia. Quickly and easily prepared, the different ways to cook them are so numerous it would be hard to find someone who did not like them in one form or another. Favorite Chinese foods are crisp snow peas, crunchy water chestnuts, crisply fried chicken, duck braised with cinnamon and star anise, and dried mushrooms simmered with ginger and soy sauce. *Hokkien mee* soup, noodle soup; *Choon pia*, spring rolls with a touch of cinnamon; *Yong tau foo*, stuffed bean curd; *Char Kway Teow*, fried noodles mixed with pork, sausage slices, shrimp, or squid with beaten eggs; *Taukwa Tauceo*, spicy bean curd in salted soybean paste; *Ban chan kuay*, light and puffy sweet pancakes, filled with chopped peanuts and sesame seeds; and *Teochew*, congee, a rice porridge eaten for breakfast, are other staple dishes in their extensive repertoire. Seasonings, used with discretion, are hot oil, oyster sauce, star anise, soy sauce, five spice powder, fermented beans, and salted soybeans.

Indian cuisine is based on the intricate blending of fragrant spices, such as cumin, turmeric, chili peppers, and curry leaves. Not all of the spices used are hot. The sweeter spices, such as cardamom, nutmeg, clove, and cinnamon, are mild. Indians scorn the curry powder used in Europe and America. Their freshly ground curry spices are specific to each food, and may be fiery or mild, generously or gently spiced, depending on the dish. Indian cooks add to these complex spice blends a variety of roots and herbs that further intrigue the taste buds. As in Thailand, Malaysians often buy their spices from a spice merchant who grinds and blends them to order. Curries cooked by Malaysian cooks have a very different flavor than those cooked in India. Fresh lemongrass, star anise, and even soy sauce add unusual and distinctive tastes. India's wonderful vegetarian food, created from varied combinations of tubers, fruits, bean curd, dried beans, lentils, and leafy greens, is unique. One famous Indian dish, served in all Indian eating shops, is *Murtaba*, a square, curry-filled pancake made with an extremely thin sheet of dough. It is fun to watch the vendor fling the ball of oiled dough into the air, continually twirling it to stretch the dough to the thinnest sheet possible. Dropped onto an extremely hot griddle, it cooks rapidly while the vendor dollops curried lamb or chicken onto the steaming pancake. In seconds it is folded and served to the waiting customer. *Gulai Telor*, a spicy Muslim Indian dish, is made with eggs, potatoes, prawns, and cuttlefish in a sweet, spicy sauce; *nasi kanda*, beef curry and fish curry with hard-cooked eggs; *dosa*, a fried split pea pancake. *Korma* and *Biriani* are two dishes from India that Malays have expropriated— *Korma*, spicy lamb with yogurt and saffron, and *Biriani*, rice flavored with saffron, cardamom, and cinnamon. Indian breads are famous the world over. In Malaysia, Indian shops specializing in breads are called

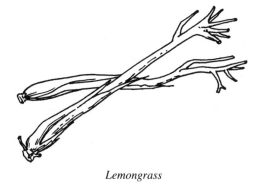

Lemongrass

roti canai, named for an extremely popular unleavened bread. A satis-fying breakfast at a *roti canai* is bread smothered in curry sauce. There are many banana leaf curry shops serving spicy meat, fish, or vegetar-ian curries. Banana leaves substitute for plates, hence their name. Everything is eaten with the fingers at banana leaf curry shops, using balls of rice to maneuver the food, and also to mop up sauces.

Penang: Pearl of the Orient

Despite the fast-paced crowded towns, half of the population of Malaysia are engaged in agricultural pursuits, living in villages that until this century were largely cut off from one another. Linked today to their closest towns by miles of paved road, goods and services are much easier to come by and the villagers no longer need to be as self-sufficient as they once were. Increasingly, young people seek wider horizons, leaving their families to make their way in the major cities. Nevertheless, Malaysia is still a country of sleepy *kampongs* (villages), gorgeous beaches, jungles, and rice paddies. All of these can be found on the beautiful island of Penang, lying off the coast of peninsular Malaysia, just south of the Thai border. Though Penang is now linked to the mainland by a bridge, people continue to take the ferry, which plies a circuitous route between the flotillas of freighters docked at the thriving port of Georgetown. Penang is known as the "pearl of the orient." One of the great curiosities here is the water villages. Built on stilts embedded in the sand, they are inhabited by fishermen and other watermen. At high tide the villages perch above the water. At low tide the fishermen's boats may be seen beached on the exposed sand below the houses. Wooden planking substitutes for sidewalks. Each pier thrusting out to sea is owned by a different clan. Walking on another clan's pier is forbidden and will get the trespasser doused, at the very least. Georgetown, the pretty capital of the island, named after Britain's King George III, has a definite Chinese flavor, though splendid colonial buildings and an old fort left by the British are still evident. A *padang* (green) is the focal point of the city. Georgetown boasts many fine Buddhist temples, including the Temple of Paradise, the biggest in Malaysia. One curious Chinese temple has live vipers coiled around branches above the altar. Fortunately they are only lethal if disturbed! The streets of the old town are narrow and filled with Chinese shophouses, selling goods from Europe and America as well as Thailand and India. No one seems keen to go to sleep on Penang—bars, nightclubs, and restaurants remain open at all hours, and foodstalls and roving vendors sell their spicy concoctions to hungry revelers until dawn.

Hotels and restaurants along Penang's superb beaches specialize in delicious freshly caught seafood. Penang is famous for Nonya cooking, which evolved from the intermarriage of *babas* (Chinese men) and *nonyas* (Malayan women) in the Straits settlements of Penang, Malacca, and Singapore. When Chinese men, in the early 1800s, came to Malaya to work in the settlements in Malacca, Penang, and Singapore, they were not allowed to bring Chinese women with them. Eventually, the men took Malay wives. New Chinese settlers married daughters from the first Chinese/Malay alliances, and today their descendants are almost pure Chinese. The distinctive cuisine, called Nonya, evolved from these Peranakan, Straits Chinese. Nonya food is a blending of Chinese and Malayan ingredients, using Chinese techniques. All the ingredients needed to prepare authentic Chinese food are on hand in a Nonya kitchen, but not all Nonya ingredients are found in a Chinese kitchen. For centuries the recipes and techniques for this unusual cuisine were passed from mother or grandmother to daughter. Nothing was written down. Without guidance from their mothers-in-law, young wives were hard-pressed to produce their husband's favorite childhood dishes. Malacca's Nonya cooking is sweeter than Penang's. The sour taste preferred by the people of

Penang is achieved through liberal use of lime and tamarind. Spring rolls are flavored with soy sauce and cinnamon. Ginger flowers are eaten in a chicken salad, tossed with fresh shrimp, and topped with a sour dressing. Nonya cooking has some wonderful curries and perfectly delicious desserts and cakes. One famous Nonya treat is homemade sausage. Nowadays many young Straits Chinese prefer eating out to spending their time working in the kitchen, and restaurants are gaining in popularity. Street vendors too are doing a lively trade. Lunch, for busy office workers, is often bought at a foodstall on the way to work. *Nasi lemak*, coconut-flavored rice with shrimp, fried fish, crisp vegetable slices, and a fiery dollop of *sambal*, is easily portable when wrapped in a banana leaf.

South of Georgetown the bustle stops, and the quiet existence of the *kampongs* soothes the soul. Unchanged for centuries, simple houses are constructed so that the living quarters are well above ground level. Placed at the foot of the steps leading to the entrance is a basin of water for foot-washing. Cleanliness, one of the tenets in the Koran, is strictly followed and the Muslim houses are spanking clean inside and out. The surrounding gardens grow fruit trees, vegetables, and flowers. Further south, rice paddies gleam in the sun. Plantations intersperse the thick jungle in the northern, hilly part of the island, growing nutmeg, clove, and pepper. Along the less populated east coast of the peninsula, seasonal changes dictate the lives of the fishing community as they have for centuries. Stout barriers of woven palm leaves are erected along the shoreline against monsoon winds. Unable to set sail during the three months of bad weather, fishermen move their weatherbeaten fishing huts further inland and wait out the time repairing their nets, refurbishing their brightly painted boats, and visiting their families. The seas around Malaysia teem with fish and shellfish—a significant part of the Malaysian diet. The east coast of the peninsula is not as prosperous as the west. Populated almost exclusively by Muslim Malays, they prefer to lead lives based on their traditional Islamic beliefs.

Uninhabited islands off the eastern coast offer unspoiled beaches, coconut groves, and dazzling coral reefs with unparalleled marine life. Parrot fish, angel fish, striped and spotted fish in every hue, colorful anemones and giant clams, make their home near the reef. During the season when seas are calm, female turtles with mottled dark green shells, measuring six feet across, come ashore at night to bury their eggs in the sand. Ungainly on land, the lumbering leatherback turtles laboriously dig a hole, and lay their eggs in it one by one. Dozens of female turtles struggle up the sandy beach each night, and each one lays about a hundred eggs. Considered a great delicacy, the round fat eggs command a high market price. Government officers guard the beaches at egg-laying time to fill government hatcheries. The law allows fishermen to collect the eggs when officials are not in the vicinity, but, to prevent extinction, stipulates that 50 percent of the turtle eggs be taken to the hatcheries, where they are kept secure until they hatch. The baby turtles, released on the beach, totter straight for the sea. The ocean floor around Malaysia and Indonesia is littered with the wrecks of sunken ships from earlier times, when warring kingdoms and pirate ships fought to the death on the high seas. Underwater exploration in search of these wrecks, reputed to be loaded with treasure, is spawning a new industry.

The Steaming Jungles of East Malaysia

In East Malaysia, 70 percent of Sabah's rolling hills and valleys are covered in jungle. Mount Kinabalu, the highest peak in Malaysia, is here, and also the state capital, Kota Kinabalu. The Kadazan tribe inhabiting the jungle near Mount Kinabalu live in palm-thatched villages, amid rain forests teeming with wildlife destined for the cooking pot. Nuts, roots, wild fruits, and herbal medicines are also collected in the rain forests. Men do the hunting and fishing. Women grow sago in village plots and help tend the rice fields. Cooking methods are uncomplicated—steaming, boiling, and grilling over charcoal. An iron pot filled with a savory stew of oxtail or chicken will be found hanging above the charcoal embers all day. The Kadazans do not observe set mealtimes, eating whenever they are hungry. Abundant foods, such as fish, are pickled or preserved.

A deserted village, outside the small town of Madai in Sabah, becomes a hotbed of activity twice a year when swifts fly in to build nests in large limestone caves next to the village. These birds' nests are the central ingredient in a delicate tasting soup, renowned in all Chinese communities the world over. To reach the nests, villagers climb ladders and bamboo platforms to dizzying heights. White nests are more valuable than black, selling for $500 per pound in the markets of Hong Kong. There are several of these outcroppings of limestone in Borneo. One famous site in the Niah Caves National Park, in Sarawak, has yielded archaeological proof that, as early as 700 A.D., the Niahan people traded birds' nests and hornbill ivory for Chinese porcelain and beads. Swifts by the millions inhabit these caves today. Their nests are the most flavorful and the most expensive in Borneo. Though collecting is very dangerous work, the whereabouts of high-yield caves are kept secret and this information is passed from father to son.

Sarawak is the largest state in Malaysia. Kuching, the state capital, has architecture reflecting its colonial past. Many Chinese make their home in Kuching. All restaurants and other eating places serve southern Chinese dishes. Over 70 percent of the state is covered in rain forest. Pepper cultivation began in peninsular Malaysia in 1619. At that time vines were trained to climb on living trees—today tall stakes are used. Women and young boys gather the berries. Green peppercorns are dropped after harvesting into a vat of brine. The rest are spread out to dry in the sun. It takes three days for them to turn black. White peppercorns have been stripped of their pericarps before drying. Sarawak is the world's largest exporter of peppercorns. Pepper cultivation, started in Singapore in the early 1900s, dwindled with the advent of rubber plantations. Seasoning food is but one of pepper's uses. Varieties irritating enough to cause injury are mixed with the poison used to coat the tips of darts and arrows. Many tales are told of the fierce headhunting tribes of Borneo with their poison-tipped arrows and their penchant for human flesh. Fortunately, headhunting is now outlawed, and the occasional skull seen hanging from the rafters is certainly a family heirloom. Animist beliefs co-exist with Christian values. But in some instances old customs die hard. Women of the Kenyah Dayak tribe here from infancy wear heavy, decorative weights through their earlobes to stretch them. Lobes that reach well below shoulder level are not uncommon.

Longhouses are famous here. Though tribal patterns of living differ, they all prefer to stay in their communal longhouses, resisting the government's efforts to move them to more conventional dwellings. Each longhouse is home to an entire tribe. They choose a headman to govern the group. The longhouse is divided into separate family areas, each with its own kitchen. A huge open veranda runs the length of the building in front, another narrower one in back is used for storing jars of fermented foods, for drying rice and other foods. The front veranda is a communal area where guests are entertained, and meetings and all tribal ceremonies are held. A large attic affords extra sleeping space, and houses a loom and tools used for making crafts. Handwoven blankets, baskets of rattan and bamboo, sometimes beautifully decorated with beadwork, earn extra income for the tribes. Longhouses are always built on stilts next to a river, which is used daily for washing and fishing. The river is the main transportation route, keeping each longhouse in touch with its neighbors up or down stream. Hospitable and generous, the tribes people welcome visitors. Most longhouses are completely self-sufficient, growing rice, vegetables, and fruit in plots next to their dwellings. Cash crops, such as cocoa or sago, are produced to sell on market day. Markets afford isolated tribal groups a regular meeting place. Hilltribe people bearing baskets of produce, and fishermen their catch, congregate each Sunday in rural towns to buy and sell and catch up on the news.

Malaysia's tropical climate is ideal for growing vegetables. Some of the more unusual varieties used routinely are bitter melon, shaped like a cucumber with a ridged skin; cassava root with a brown bark that is peeled and cooked when young and ground into flour when mature; *kencur* which is a type of ginger; long beans; and a long-leaved aquatic plant with a mild flavor, similar to spinach. Several of these vegetables are found in Asian markets in America. Malaysia is also blessed with a bounty of tropical fruits. In addition to the usual wide variety of bananas, succulent pineapple, and rosy papaya, Malaysia grows wonderful durian, considered the king of fruits. The eagerly awaited durian season turns the usually easygoing, unflappable Malaysians into fanatics. Beside the motorways, foodstalls displaying the first crop of durians stop traffic. People leave their cars to hunker-down and discuss the merits of each specimen. The skin is pored over for any blemishes or cracks, the color noted, and the fruit gently shaken to see if the seeds are loose—a sign of ripeness. Connoisseurs, and serious about their durians, they want only the best, which includes getting the most pungent and smelly ones. Eating the ambrosial creamy fruit has been likened to eating peaches and cream in an outhouse! Nevertheless, durian addicts happily consume them by the dozen. Growing on tall forest trees, durians are not harvested like other fruits, but left to fall to the ground when ripe. During the season, owners need to keep an eye on their trees or they would certainly lose their crop—elephants and tigers are known to covet the odiferous treat. Durian, and the purple mangosteen with its neat, snowy segments that pop out as soon as you squeeze the fruit, ripen at the same time of year, and are often eaten together. Malaysians designate the durian as a "heating" fruit and the mangosteen as a "cooling" fruit. Alcohol is also the epitome of a "heating" food and to drink alcohol with durian is to court disaster. Hairy red rambutans, golden and white mangoes, guava, passion fruit, and numerous citrus fruits are abundant. A different type of durian without the prickles and the smell is soursop. True to its name, it has a sour tang and makes a refreshing juice. Star fruit's two varieties, one much sweeter than the other, are also great thirst quenchers. The sourer star fruit is delicious in salads. Huge jackfruit are often sliced and fried and, of course, unripe bananas are used frequently in Southeast Asian cooking. Banana is one of the biggest items in the international fruit trade, and the world consumes more of them than any other fruit. A banana plant is actually an herb with an underground stem. Above ground the trunk is composed of tightly overlapping leaf sheaths and is called

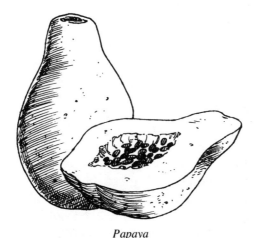

Papaya

Durian

a pseudostem. The heavy, dark red flower bud is used in cooking. Bananas are chockful of vitamins and minerals, fat-free, rich in fiber, and provide a substantial slow release of energy. At a mere 70 calories per average-sized banana, it's no wonder they top the list of the fruit consumed the most around the globe.

One of the most important utensils in a Malaysian kitchen is the *kuali* or wok. Made from iron, it is heavier than the one used in Chinese cookery. The *kuali* is not suitable for dishes cooked with coconut milk or cream as the iron interacts with the milk and causes discoloring. Enamel pans are used instead. Various sizes of coconut shell spoons and dippers are prevalent. A big frying pan, a good-sized steamer, the all-important mortar and pestle, and a grinding stone are standard items in a Malaysian kitchen.

Singapore

Southern Nonya food is synonymous with Singapore. Basic to Nonya cooking are numerous spices, chilies, spring onions, lemongrass, and pungent roots, pounded to just the right consistency in a mortar and pestle. This *rempah* is cooked in oil for a few minutes before being stirred into the other ingredients. Nonya cooks are very proud of their skill when it comes to pounding spices. It is said that an experienced cook can tell from listening to the rhythm of the pounding, whether the person is a good cook or not, and from the sound made by the pestle which spice is being pulverized. A Nonya cook will use Malay spices, coconut milk, and *sambals* (dipping sauces) to create her dishes, but adds less chili, peppercorns, and turmeric than would a Malay cook. Nevertheless, Nonya food is spicy compared to Chinese food. Rich with coconut milk, it incorporates roots, such as turmeric, ginger, and galangal, as well as aromatic leaves and *belacan* (shrimp paste). Nonya cooks have developed a line of sweet desserts and cakes from glutinous rice, Malaccan palm sugar and syrup, and freshly grated coconut and coconut cream. A particular favorite is *naga sari*, a soft white jellylike pudding made of mung beans, sugar, and coconut milk. Nonya cooking is considerably sweeter and milder than Malay cooking.

The ethnic foods of the three races have also intermingled to produce a cuisine incredibly rich in variety and innovation. Singaporean Malays eat noodles doused with curry sauce, Indians perfume their curries with star anise and lemongrass, and the Chinese happily consume quantities of Malay satays. Originally from Indonesia, satays are undoubtedly Singapore's favorite dish, served with rice cakes, wrapped in banana leaves. Thousands of charcoal fires all over the city, from dusk to dawn, waft the scent of grilling meat, chicken, and shrimp into the night air. At dusk the food vendors come into their own. Parking lots turn into food markets at the close of the business day. Lights are strung up, tables and chairs set out, and in the twin-

Coconut ladle

kling of an eye every wok in sight sizzles with one or another of the savory, tempting dishes of Chinese noodles, Indian curries, or Javanese fried rice. Vegetarian specialties are much in demand, as are fresh fish and shellfish dishes. Luscious tropical fruits assuage the palate at the end of the meal.

Singaporeans are passionate about food; they discuss it endlessly and with unflagging interest. Word of a newly created dish spreads with lightning speed. Singaporeans are not snobbish about their eating establishments. The creativity of a new foodstall cook is just as gladly hailed as one in an air-conditioned temple of gastronomy. Culinary curiosity transcends class boundaries, and it is not uncommon to see a well-heeled customer in a chauffeur-driven Mercedes pull up to a humble foodstall reputed to have the best noodle dish in town. A certain amount of discomfort for a taste of something special is par for the course. The standard of cooking is extremely high in Singapore. Whether it is Chinese, Nonya, Malayan, Sumatran, Javanese, Indian, Thai, Japanese, or Western, you can be sure it will be cooked better in Singapore.

Singapore is an island nation, situated at the tip of the Malay peninsula. The main island and the city of Singapore, with 57 smaller islands, covers 240 square miles (386 square kilometers). Singapore lies closer to the equator than any other city in Southeast Asia. Its temperature is invariably in the low eighties, and outbursts of torrential rain, though short-lived, occur frequently, dumping 93 inches of rain on the islands each year. The jungle and beaches that surround the city are often little more than swamps. The name Singapore derives from the Sanskrit word for lion, though there are no lions on the island and never have been. Legend tells us that the name was given to the island by a visiting Sultan whose aide mistook a fleeing tiger for a lion.

When Sir Stamford Raffles, a British East India Company official, arrived in Singapore in January 1819, he found a run-down village of about a hundred Malay shacks, surrounded by marshy jungle. He was the first to realize Singapore's potential. Its strategic position astride sea lanes that connect the Middle East and Asia made it an ideal trading post, and the settlement grew rapidly. Raffles's vision is responsible for the present-day plan of the city, which has separate districts assigned to each ethnic group. Raffles took complete control, supervising all aspects of its development. He even managed to abolish gambling for the length of his tenure. Ill health forced him to leave Singapore in 1823. In 1824 Singapore officially became a British colony. Today the areas of Chinatown, Little India, and the Arab Street Area are very little changed. Some of the original Peranakan, Straits Chinese houses can be seen in Singapore. Painted in vivid colors, with Chinese tiled roofs and lintels carved by Malayan craftsmen, these houses are richly decorated inside and out.

Singapore gained its independence and became a republic in 1965. Since then the country has surged ahead to achieve one of the highest standards of living in Southeast Asia. Singapore is booming, and its growth rate, high technological skills, gleaming high-rise office blocks, oil refineries, and bustling port lined with foreign freighters and tankers, are impressive. Japanese vehicles crowd the thoroughfares, along with Mercedes and BMWs. Clean, orderly, with pristine parks lush with beautiful greenery, Singapore even manages not to have rush-hour traffic jams. All this was accomplished by dictates from Lee Kuan Yew, Singapore's former Prime Minister, now Senior Minister. An authoritarian, he got his point across to the populace with the aid of slogans, exhorting all citizens to be well-behaved: not to litter, nor spit in public, nor wear their hair long (this one for men only), to be courteous while driving, more sanitary, and well-mannered at home and at work. Fines for not obeying the rules are astronomical—$600 for littering, $300 for eating in the subway.

The Malayan, Chinese, and Indian descendants of the original settlers have intermingled today to the point where a genuine Singaporean culture has evolved. Intermarriage is still rare, especially for Muslim Malays. Nevertheless, there is much common ground among the races and a definite national identity. The population is just over 3 million, 78 percent of whom are third- and fourth-generation Straits Chinese, 14 percent are Malays, and 7 percent are Indian. The majority refer to themselves as Singaporeans. Mandarin is vigorously encouraged as the unifying language for Chinese. Tamil is the official Indian language, and Malay is the national language of the republic.

Some of the best Indian food is to be found in *Tandoori* restaurants. Tandoori specialties are marinated in spices before being cooked in a vat-shaped clay oven, heated with charcoal. The intense heat inside will cook a small chicken in 10 minutes. A long skewer, with the bird impaled on it, is thrust through an opening into the oven. The searing heat seals in the juices, and the chicken emerges crisp-skinned and wonderfully succulent. Tandoori chicken is the most famous, but other meats, fish, lentils, and breads, too, are cooked in the tandoor. Some of the beautifully spiced Indian specialties are juicy chunks of lamb, simmered with fennel seeds and curry spices, served with creamy yogurt; yogurt, lemon, and ground cumin dressing for a soothing cucumber salad, called *raita*; and *biriani*, a saffron rice dish, studded with toasted nuts, seeds, and dried fruits. *Dal*, a side dish, is made with red lentils, simmered with cinnamon sticks and plenty of bay leaves. Delicately spiced prawn curries and richly spiced chicken curries are perennial favorites, as are the many vegetable curries, garnished with crisply fried, minced onion and garlic. Not to be missed are the many fragrant Indian breads hot from the oven.

With the large number of Chinese in Singapore, naturally the most famous of China's regional cuisines are well-represented. Szechuan restaurants, redolent of five spice powder, serve fiery foods laced with finely ground Szechuan peppercorns. The Szechuan peppercorn actually bears no relationship to the pepper vine. Intensely flavored Szechuan peppercorns are the dried red flower and tiny seed of the prickly ash tree that grows wild in Asia. Dried leaves from this tree are ground into a spice beloved of the Japanese, called *Sancho. Kimone*, pickled ash tree leaves, is also widely used in Japan. Szechuan peppercorns are one of the ingredients in five spice powder. The others are star anise, fennel, cinnamon bark, and cloves. Proximity to the Malays has engendered in the Singaporean Chinese a taste for a little spice in their food. Hot *sambals* are served with Chinese fish dishes, chilies find their way into spring rolls, and pickled green chilies frequently grace Chinese dinner tables.

Another cuisine that has influenced the cooking in Singapore is *Nasi Padang*. *Nasi Padang* food is intensely hot. Originating in West Sumatra, renowned for some of the hottest food in the world, most of these fiery dishes are curries cooked with lots of chili, spices, and coconut cream. *Nasi Padang* restaurants in Singapore display their repertoire of cooked dishes in the restaurant window so that people can point out which ones they wish to sample. The food, served in separate small bowls, arrives all at the same time. The cost of the meal is computed from the number of empty bowls on the table.

Malayan food also has its devotees in Singapore, particularly among Muslims, and there are several restaurants serving Javanese food, which in turn is influenced by the cooking of Sumatra and Madura.

Though forks and spoons are provided for diners in Singapore, the traditional way to eat food is with the fingers of the right hand, using rice, lightly kneaded with the fingertips, to maneuver the food. Many Southeast Asians prefer to use the fingers to put food in their mouths, and feel that the flavor of the food is impaired by using utensils. Short-handled Chinese porcelain spoons accompany bowls of soup and dinner plates are used for Nonya food. Coffee, rather than tea, is the preferred beverage with Nonya meals. Alcohol is seldom served at mealtimes. In a Singaporean home, all the dishes, including the rice and soup, are put on the table at the same time, and everyone helps themselves with a little from this or that dish.

In Singapore every kitchen will almost certainly have a modern gas stove. Most people have updated their houses inside and out. The kitchen will be equipped with a wok or *kuali* for stir-frying. Regular saucepans are used for simmering foods and making soups. Sharp cleavers and knives are a necessity, as is a chopping block, a mortar and pestle, a grinding stone for pulverizing spices and roots, and a grater for grating coconut. In an American kitchen, most of these functions can be duplicated with a food processor.

Wok

Recipes from Malaysia

Shrimp and Watercress Soup

½ lb.	shrimp, shelled and deveined
1	bunch of watercress
2 T.	peanut oil
2 large	shallots, sliced
1	garlic clove, minced
2	fresh hot chilies, seeded and sliced
½ t.	turmeric
1 t.	sea salt
3 C.	fish broth, preferably homemade OR
1½ C.	clam juice diluted with water
1½ C.	coconut milk, canned

Cut shrimp into half-inch slices and refrigerate. Snip off watercress leaves. Coarsely chop watercress stems and set both aside. Heat oil in a heavy-bottomed saucepan, and stir-fry the shallots until golden over medium heat. Stir in garlic, chilies, and turmeric and continue to stir-fry for 2 minutes. Add watercress stems and salt and stir-fry for a minute or two, then pour in fish broth and simmer for 5 minutes. Add watercress leaves and coconut milk and simmer 2 minutes. Just before serving, reheat soup, add shrimp, and when soup returns to the simmer, remove from heat and serve immediately.   *Serves 4*

Lightly Spiced Shiitake and Button Mushrooms

1–2 oz.	dried shiitake mushrooms
2 T.	peanut oil
2	shallots, minced
1	thin quarter-sized slice of fresh ginger
¼ T.	ground turmeric
1	jalapeno pepper, sliced
½	red bell pepper, sliced
10 oz.	fresh button mushrooms, peeled and halved
1 T.	fish sauce
½ t.	sea salt

Shiitake mushrooms

¼ lb.   fresh snow peas
        cilantro for garnish

Soak shiitake mushrooms in half a cup of warm water for 30 minutes, or place shiitake and a quarter cup of water in a microwave-safe bowl, cover with wrap, and microwave for 3 minutes. Drain reserving liquid and wash shiitakes thoroughly. Set aside. Heat oil in a wok, and stir-fry shallots, ginger, and turmeric over medium-high heat for 2 or 3 minutes. Add jalapeno, bell pepper, shiitake, button mushrooms, fish sauce, and salt. Stir-fry for 2 minutes to mix thoroughly. Lower heat, cover wok, and simmer for 2 minutes more. Uncover wok, add snow peas, and stir-fry over medium-high heat for barely 30 seconds. The snow peas should stay very crisp as a foil to the soft mushrooms.

Serves 4

Grilled Red Snapper with Spicy Soy Sauce

1 whole   red snapper, weighing about 2 lb.
1 T.   sea salt
3 T.   lime juice
⅓ C.   soy sauce
2 T.   brown sugar
1   thinly sliced hot red chili pepper

2   grindings of black pepper
1 T.   peanut oil for grill
1   sliced scallion for garnish
          cilantro leaves for garnish

Mix together 2 tablespoons of lime juice with the sea salt, and rub all over the fish. Allow to marinate for 20 minutes. Wash fish, and pat dry with paper towels. In a small bowl, mix together the remaining lime juice, soy sauce, sugar, chili pepper, and black pepper. Preheat broiler, brush grill with oil, and broil fish for 10 minutes per inch of thickness, turning once. Baste fish two to three times per side with the soy mixture. Remove fish to a warm platter to serve, and garnish with scallions and cilantro leaves. Pass remaining soy mixture separately.

Serves 2–3

Rojak *Fruit and* Vegetable *Salad* with *Sweet-Tart* Dressing

Dressing

1 t.   dried shrimp paste
1 T. Chinese rice wine vinegar
1 t.   Chinese chili paste with garlic
1 T. sugar
½ t. salt
3 T. fresh lime juice

Wrap shrimp paste in foil and grill for about 8 minutes, turning once. Dissolve shrimp paste in rice wine vinegar. Stir in Chinese chili paste, sugar, and salt. Set aside.

Salad

1 T. sesame seeds, toasted
¼ C. raw peanuts
1   thin, seedless cucumber, peeled and cut into matchsticks
1   ripe guava, peeled, seeded, and cut into bite-sized pieces
1   Asian pear, peeled, seeded, and cut into bite-sized pieces
1   star fruit, sliced crosswise
1   mango, peeled and cubed

½   pineapple—not too ripe, peeled, cored, and cubed
1   thinly sliced, small red chili, seeded and chopped
3 T.   fresh lime juice

Spread raw peanuts on a baking sheet and roast in a 325°F oven for 10 minutes. Cool and rub off skins. Chop coarsely and set aside.

In a salad bowl, toss fruits and vegetables with lime juice to prevent discoloration. Stir in the shrimp paste dressing and toss well. Sprinkle with the sesame seeds and peanuts and serve at once.

Serves 4–6

Recipes from Singapore

Roast Chicken

6 lb.   roasting chicken

Paste

6–8   dried red chilies
1 T.   fennel seeds
½ t.   cumin seeds
1 T.   ground turmeric
1 t.   sea salt
⅓ C.   fresh cilantro leaves
           1-inch cube of fresh ginger, sliced
6 large   shallots, sliced
3   garlic cloves, crushed
1   stalk lemongrass, minced
⅔ C.   canned coconut milk

Soak chilies for 20 minutes. Grind fennel and cumin seeds in a spice grinder and mix with ground turmeric and salt. Using a food processor, make a paste with the chilies, spice mixture, cilantro, ginger, shallots, garlic, and lemongrass. Mix paste thoroughly into coconut milk and rub this mixture over the chicken—inside and out. Let chicken marinate, refrigerated, for 30 minutes. Remove from refrigerator and continue to marinate for 30 minutes longer. Preheat oven to 300°F. Place chicken on a rack in a large roasting pan and roast for 2½ hours or until the leg juices run clear when pricked with a fork. Remove to a warm platter and let rest for 10 minutes.

Serves 6

Shrimp in Spicy Bean Sauce

12	oz.	fresh shrimp, peeled and deveined
½	t.	salt
½	t.	freshly grated ginger
1		garlic clove, finely minced
1	T.	Chinese rice wine
1		fresh red chili pepper
1		fresh tiny green chili pepper
1	T.	fermented black beans
1–2	t.	Chinese chili and garlic sauce
2	t.	hoisin sauce
2	T.	peanut oil
2		scallions, sliced
2	T.	fresh cilantro leaves

Shell shrimp and mix thoroughly with the garlic, salt, ginger, and rice wine. Marinate for 30 minutes. Seed chili peppers and slice finely. Rinse black beans, chop them coarsely, and mix them with chili sauce and hoisin sauce. Heat 1½ tablespoons of oil in wok and stir-fry chili peppers for a second or two—do not let them burn—add shrimp with marinade and stir-fry for 2–3 minutes, or until shrimp are pink and opaque. Add remaining oil and black bean mixture, stir-fry, coating the shrimp well with the sauce, for about 30 seconds longer. Serve immediately garnished with cilantro leaves and scallions.

Serves 2–3

Green Papaya Salad

⅓	C.	peanuts
1		small, firm papaya, seeded and grated
1		carambola (star fruit), thinly sliced crosswise
½		Asian Pear, cored and cut into bite-sized pieces
2		Italian tomatoes, seeded and diced

Carambola

3	T.	fresh lime juice
1		small hot red chili, seeded and thinly sliced
1		shallot, finely sliced
1	T.	fish sauce
3–4	T.	whole cilantro leaves

Roast peanuts in a 350°F oven for 10 minutes. Cool, rub off skins, chop coarsely, and set aside. In a glass serving bowl, lightly toss grated papaya, carambola, and tomatoes with the lime juice. Add chili, scallions, and fish sauce and toss again. Sprinkle with chopped peanuts and decorate with whole cilantro leaves.   *Serves 4*

Singapore Chicken in Coconut Milk with Ginger

3	lb.	boned chicken breasts
2	T.	butter
½	C.	grated fresh coconut
2	medium	onions, sliced
1	t.	ground star anise
2	t.	ground coriander seed
½	t.	saffron, soaked for 10 minutes in water
2		garlic cloves, minced
2	thick	slices of ginger, peeled

I	fresh chili pepper, seeded and sliced; wear rubber gloves
I small	stalk of lemongrass
3 T.	fresh lime juice
I T.	hoisin sauce
I t.	salt
1½ C.	coconut milk

Cut chicken breasts into one-inch pieces and refrigerate. In a large wok, over medium heat, melt butter and stir-fry grated coconut until beginning to color. Push to the side and stir-fry onions for 3 minutes. Set aside. In a mini food processor, make a paste from the star anise, coriander seed, saffron, garlic, ginger, chili pepper, lemongrass, lime juice, hoisin sauce, and salt. Over high heat, stir into the wok the spice paste, the chicken pieces, and the coconut milk. As soon as the mixture starts to boil, reduce heat and cook, stirring for about 6–8 minutes, or until the chicken is cooked. Serve immediately with rice.   *Serves 6*

Fried Banana Cakes Nonya Style

4	very ripe bananas
I t.	finely grated lime zest
½–⅔ C.	flour (depending on size and moistness of fruit)
¼ t.	baking powder
	pinch of salt
I t.	sugar
	lime wedges
	sugar for sprinkling or syrup
	corn oil for deep-frying

Peel and mash bananas. Stir in lime zest. Sift together the flour, baking powder, and salt. Put mashed bananas into a mixing bowl and work in flour mixture a little at a time to form a soft dough. Knead for a minute or two to lighten the dough. Heat oil—it should be about one-half inch deep—and fry small, flat cakes of dough, turning to brown evenly. Drain on paper towel, sprinkle with sugar, and serve hot with lime wedges.   *Makes 12–18 cakes*

INDONESIA

Indonesian food is as diverse and exciting as the people who live on this 3,200 mile (5,150 kilometer) long archipelago of over 13,000 islands. Less than 1,000 islands are inhabited, and thousands of the others are too small to inspire names. Borneo, on the other hand, is the third biggest island in the world, and Sumatra the fifth. Of the 13,677 islands that make up Indonesia, the five biggest are Sumatra, Java, Kalimantan (Borneo), Sulawesi, and Irian Jaya (Dutch New Guinea). Sumatra is the most westerly. The narrow Straits of Malacca separate Sumatra from the Malay peninsula. Irian Jaya is the most easterly. Australia's closest neighbor, it shares the huge island of New Guinea with independent Papua Guinea. The archipelago stretches from the Indian Ocean well into the Pacific. Situated in the part of the Pacific called The Ring of Fire, Indonesia's 70–80 active volcanoes average 10 destructive eruptions annually. Krakatoa's serene shape, halfway between West Java and Sumatra's southern tip, belies the gigantic volcanic explosion of 1883, which sent 90-foot tidal waves across thousands of miles of ocean. The debris, millions of tons of it, altered global climate patterns throughout the ensuing decade.

Volcanic soils are extremely fertile. Java and Bali are blessed with some of the most fertile soil on earth. Their soil is said to be so rich that a man who builds a wooden fence will have a thriving hedge in six months. The name Sumatra means black earth: black from the lava spewed over the island from centuries of volcanic eruptions. The fertility of the soil is legendary. Nourishing the peoples of Indonesia for over 500,000 years, it has attracted wave after wave of Malay settlers. Indians followed in the second century A.D. The cultures of these and other early peoples are preserved in the wealth of archaeological remains in present-day Indonesia. Fragmented and multicultured, Indonesia has 300 ethnic groups and over 250 spoken dialects. The official language, and the one taught in schools, is Bahasa Indonesia. The western islands, which were once joined to Indo-China, were settled by Asiatic nomads. Several of the easterly islands, originally connected to a land mass running north to south, were linked to Australia, and were settled by dark-skinned nomads from the antipodes. These land bridges account for the multiplicity of ethnic groups, and differences in flora and fauna between the island groups. Indonesia is at the crossroads of the great trade routes that link the Middle East and Asia. Indian traders, as early as the fifth century, set up trading posts on Sumatra, in the Malacca Straits, to protect their ships from the monsoon winds. The trading posts soon spread to Java and Borneo. Indians settled to proselytize their Buddhist and Hindu religions. In the eleventh century, Arabs brought Islam. The Spanish and Portuguese introduced Roman Catholicism in the sixteenth century, and the English and Dutch their various Protestant sects in the seventeenth century. Today, although Muslims predominate, there are still pockets of each of these great religions in Indonesia, some of them so thoroughly assimilated as to be almost unrecognizable. Indonesia's oldest Islamic kingdom was established in northern Sumatra.

Padang is the capital of West Sumatra. The third largest city in Indonesia, it is clean and orderly. Devoutly Muslim, appropriate dress for women is strictly enforced. More than 90 percent of the people living in Padang are ethnically descendants of the Minangkabau tribal group. Famous for their unusual architecture, the roofs of Minangkabau houses sweep upward into multiple peaks, shaped like buffalo horns. Padang's climate is intensely hot, despite having one of the heaviest rainfalls in the world. Rivers and streams lace the area, yet few bridges have been built and everyone crosses by ferry. Densely populated, West Sumatra produces tea, coffee, rubber, black pepper, and palm oil. Much of the jungle that then covered Sumatra has been pushed back by logging companies, plantation owners, and transmigrasi—resettled Indonesians from overcrowded areas such as

Java. The biggest oil and gas fields in Southeast Asia are here, as are many untapped mineral reserves, including gold and copper. Some settlements go back to the 1930s and were instituted originally by the Dutch, who ruled Indonesia for 320 years. Bali was one of the last islands in Indonesia to yield when faced with Dutch rule. In defiance, the entire Balinese Court walked boldly into Dutch gunfire in 1908, ritually committing suicide. Following the attack on Pearl Harbor, the Japanese drove the Dutch out of Indonesia. Indonesia finally attained independence at the end of the war in 1945.

Java, Sumatra's neighbor, with the capital of Jakarta on its northwestern coast, is the most populous island, housing the greater part of Indonesia's 175 million people. It is also one of the richest. A mountain range stretches from west to east across the island, its peaks towering over the plains and villages. Holiday resorts dot the cool upper reaches of these highlands. Central Java is famed for the fabulous Buddhist temple of Borobudur. For centuries the temple lay buried beneath volcanic ash, until it was stumbled upon by a colonel in the British Army in 1814. Excavation, followed by complete dismantling of the temple, was undertaken by archaeologists from all over the world. Each part was logged into a computer, the foundation strengthened, and the temple rebuilt, terrace by terrace. Visible for miles around, a statue of Buddha sits meditating on the upper terrace, as he has for 1,200 years. Borobudur predates Angkor Wat in Cambodia by three centuries. Jakarta is the most developed region of Indonesia, and the center of commerce, industry, and political life. Called the city of contrasts, Jakarta has sprawling slums cheek by jowl with soaring skyscrapers. Its city streets are thronged with sleek BMWs nosing past trudging pedicabs. In order to boost the tourist industry, Jakarta designated 1991 as "Visit Indonesia Year" and promised to have three new international hotels, several new upscale restaurants, and more entertainment.

The captivating island of Bali lies off the eastern tip of Java. Muslim merchants from Gujarat and Persia came to Java to trade, and at the same time to propagate their Islamic faith. As Islam began to take a strong hold, the Hindus living on Java fled to Bali. Always fiercely animistic, the Balinese mix these beliefs with the Hindu religion, changing it substantially. Religion permeates Balinese life. Religion is part of them, they wear it like a second skin. A very large part of their religion revolves around spiritual offerings. These run the gamut from a simple palm-frond platter holding rice and flowers, to an elaborate arrangement taking days to put together. No house, shop, or office is without its tiny shrine and stick of burning incense. Offerings are placed wherever the Balinese feel danger may lurk— beside a river, in a dark part of the forest, or even at a traffic intersection. They are convinced the essence of the offering, as it rises with the smoke, will nourish or placate the spirit. Their most important god resides at the summit of Gunung Agung, the 10,308-foot-high volcano that towers over the island. The Balinese believe that failure to placate him could bring calamity on their heads, as it has in the past.

Their religious calendar is studded with joyful festivals—several each week. People may be seen walking to the temples each carrying an exquisitely crafted offering that is often taller than the person carrying it, composed of fruit, flowers, and intricate designs made of colored rice. The offerings are stacked several rows deep outside the temple, and at the close of the religious ceremony the priests and worshippers joyously share in a gargantuan feast. Although there is no Balinese word for art, everyone is busy with either batik, painting, sculpting, classical dance, instrument making, fabric design, or fashioning exquisite jewelry and woodcarvings. There are over 2,000 dance troupes in Bali. Each village has its *gamelan* (percussion orchestra). The Balinese like their music loud, and players joyfully hammer away on the bronze bars of their instruments with wooden mallets. Gongs are the most popular. Numerous small, noisy, instruments are contrived from coconut shells. People sing at their work, and even the pigeons have whistles attached to their feet. It is small wonder that the first Dutch ship to reach Bali almost lost its crew to this happy, hospitable island. It took a full year to round them up for the return voyage!

Sulawesi, to the east, is the most mountainous island. Sheltered in this rugged terrain is the isolated Toraja tribe, known for their unique funeral ceremonies. Funerals here usually take place many months after death. Sometimes the bodies are kept in the house, wrapped in cloths, partially embalmed until the elaborate preparations for the funeral are complete. This can take months, and can cost a person's entire life savings. A thousand is not an uncommon number of guests. As all the guests need to be fed, hundreds of buffalo and other animals are slaughtered at the funeral of a very rich tribesman. After the ceremonies, the deceased is buried in deep, narrow caves in the cliffs. Funerals are festive affairs and a cause for almost delirious celebration. The Torajans are fond of meat or fish cooked with pig's blood in a bamboo tube. They also fill long bamboo tubes, at least a yard or more in length, with sap they collect through an incision in a sugar palm tree. Left to ferment for an hour or two, the sap makes a pleasant, mildly alcoholic brew.

The Fabled Spice Islands

Between Sulawesi and New Guinea are the Spice Islands of the Moluccas which, as early as 300 B.C., were known for their nutmeg and cloves. In the thirteenth century, Javanese kings, who counted the Moluccas as their own, grew hugely rich trading spices. Nutmeg, which has a flavor both spicy and sweet, has been sought after for its delicious flavor since the fifteenth century. The fruit of a tropical evergreen tree, the soft flesh surrounding the nut is used by Indonesians in desserts. Grated nutmeg is one of the most versatile of spices and its use in both sweet and savory dishes is worldwide. Covering the hard, grayish-brown nutmeg is a lacy red membrane, which, when dried and ground, yields the bright orange, pungent spice, mace. By the fifteenth century, nutmeg and cloves were much sought after in Europe and elsewhere to preserve and flavor meats, to make perfumes and lotions, and to sweeten the breath. They were essential to incense

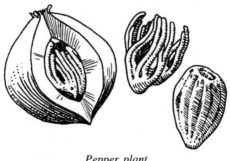

Pepper plant

used in religious ceremonies, and equally so in medicines reputed to cure stomach disorders and painful joints. Arab sultans dominated the Spice Islands (the Moluccas) from the fourteenth to the late fifteenth century. Jealously guarding the secrets of their shipping routes, both to keep the cost inflated and to discourage exploration, they spread tales of the horrendous dangers and difficulties incurred in reaching the Spice Islands. One such tale tells of a spice tree, growing in the center of a lake, guarded by fierce flesh-eating birds. Only by enticing the birds away with chunks of donkey meat could the traders sneak in and steal branches from the spice tree! As prices soared, the Dutch, hoping to gain total monopoly of the spice trade, signed a treaty with the Sultans of two of the Spice Islands, and the long colonization period in Indonesia's history began. The Dutch methods were brutal. They laid waste to spice plantations to retain the high prices, and introduced forced labor practices which endured for hundreds of years. In the early twentieth century, the monopoly was broken by the British and French who, having smuggled out seedlings of nutmeg and cloves, started competitive plantations in India and Africa. Surprisingly, cloves are no longer a part of Indonesian cooking. Instead they are used as a flavoring ingredient in tobacco, and the aroma of *krekek*—cigarettes—is pervasive.

The province of Maluka, comprising 999 islands, includes the Spice Islands. It is the only Indonesian province that has less land than water. Maluka is famous for its pristine beaches, clear water, and undersea life. When the tide goes out, exposing the reefs, groups of colorfully dressed women carrying baskets walk across the wet sand to collect delicacies from the reef. In Maluka, the change from Asian to Australian flora and fauna is very evident—kangaroos abound in the Mollucas. Indonesia is the sole habitat for two of the world's most unusual living species: the menacing Komodo Dragon, a ten-foot-long carnivorous lizard, descended from meat-eating dinosaurs who lived here 130 million years ago; and Rafflesia, an enormous, red, jungle flower which, fully opened, measures more than three feet in diameter.

The two Malaysian states, Sabah and Sarawak, cover one-quarter of Borneo. Tucked between Sarawak and Sabah is the tiny, oil-rich Sultanate of Brunei. The remainder of the huge island, Kalimantan, is laced by the rivers that constitute her major thoroughfares. In these

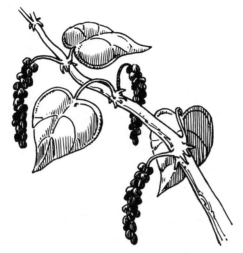

Nutmeg with mace

jungles live the fierce tribes, well known, once upon a time, as head-hunting cannibals. Many of these tribes have long since converted to Christianity. Although they still carry 6-foot-long blowpipes, and wear a quiver of poison-tipped arrows around their waists, head hunting is no longer practiced. The arrows are used to hunt game. Curiously, the poison on the arrow does not affect the meat. Until the logging companies started gnawing through it, this region was 80 percent jungle. Pepper plantations too have been carved from this densely forested terrain, so many that Indonesia is now the third largest exporter of pepper in the world. As soon as it was discovered, in the sixteenth century, that pepper preserved meats, Europeans in search of this valuable spice launched what became the Age of Discovery. A delicacy of the people of Southern Kalimantan is roast lizard. East Kalimantan is famed for its rare flora and fauna, which includes the Black Orchid. Oil revenues have boosted the economy in Balikpapan, the main gateway to the area, and the town boasts some good hotels and restaurants.

Irian Jaya is famous for its fine primitive art. The contrast between the modern coastal towns and the isolated inland village of simple wood shacks found on Irian Jaya is striking. The most inaccessible jungles are here. An alpine range, so high that planes fly between the snow-covered mountains, separates the northern part of the island from the southern. Generally speaking, the soil is fertile in the north and poor in the south, though the south does produce copra (from coconuts), rattan, and high-quality timber. Irian Jaya has rich copper deposits, gold, uranium, and Indonesia's biggest oil fields. Immense river systems, filled by Irian Jaya's incessant rainfall, course through the jungles to the south. Some of the tribes inhabiting the highlands lead lives that are scarcely different from Stone Age peoples, and many want no contact with worlds outside their own. Jayapura is the main town in the north.

Regional differences in the cooking exist among the islands of Sumatra, Java, Bali, the Mollucas, and Irian Jaya. Sumatran cooking, influenced by the Indian and Arabian foods introduced in the eleventh century, is more substantial than the cooking of the other islands. Curried beef and lamb dishes, spiced with fiery chili peppers, coriander, cumin, and lemongrass, make West Sumatran cooking some of the hottest in the world. Sumatra also has the best cooks—most of them from Padang. Nasi Padang cuisine can be found in restaurants in most cities and is usually quite expensive. The numerous dishes are often displayed in the window of the restaurant and people point to the ones they wish to sample. The traditional procedure is to have the waiter come to the table with a plethora of small dishes and the bill is calculated on the dishes consumed. This cuisine is famous for its robust flavor achieved by a skillful blending of hot spices and rich coconut cream.

Javanese cooking is more sophisticated than the robust fare of some of the other islands. It is based on a subtle blending of sweet and sour as well as hot dishes. The variety of fish and shellfish found in the oceans surrounding the islands is astounding. Catch from these waters includes huge amounts of tuna, mackerel, anchovies, and shrimp. Indonesians are also very fond of the more crawly and slithery delicacies found in the sea than are generally acceptable to Western palates. In the western part of Java, this bounty is often lightly seasoned, wrapped in a banana leaf, and steamed or grilled.

A dish often found on the menu in restaurants in the larger cities is Rijsttafel. Rijsttafel—the Dutch word for rice table—is a banquet of ten to twelve dishes, usually served in establishments that cater to foreigners. It is a throwback to the days during the Dutch occupation of Indonesia when gargantuan meals, easily comprising over one hundred dishes, were served; and servants stood ready, one at the elbow of each guest, with a morsel of banana or some other soothing tidbit, to assuage the heat from an unexpectedly hot mouthful of chili.

Java has its own feast, called a *Slametan*, to celebrate religious festivals, or births, deaths, and marriages. The centerpiece on the festive table is a huge cone of rice, decorated with fancifully carved vegetables, fruits, and flowers. Surrounding the cone is a plentiful array of delectable dishes. Indonesians are careful to provide foods that contrast with each other in flavor, texture, and temperature: spicy and mild, crisp and soft, dry and soupy, crunchy and smooth, sweet and sour, as well as dishes that are served cold, room temperature, and hot. Crispness is usually achieved in dishes such as shrimp balls, potato balls, and delicious, dried anchovy fritters by deep-frying in vegetable oils. Peanut fritters have both crunch and crispness. Noodle dishes tend to be soupy. Spices, ground to a paste, are stir-fried in a little oil, to accentuate aroma and flavor, before adding the rest of the ingredients. Coconut milk and cream smooth and thicken the sauces of Indonesia.

A famous beef dish, called Beef *Redang*, is cooked dry in a rather complicated process. First the beef and spice paste are stir-fried in oil. The coconut milk or stock is mixed in and simmered until the sauce evaporates and only the oil remains. The beef is briskly stir-fried once more in this oil, until the meat becomes completely dry and so strongly spiced that it will keep without refrigeration for a month, which is a boon for traders on their long journeys.

Bali's Varied Cuisine

A major distinction of the cuisine of Bali is the consumption of pork. There are no pork taboos for the Hindu Balinese. Roast suckling pig is a specialty here. Stuffed with spices and aromatic leaves, it is spit roasted. The crisp skin and succulent white meat are not to be missed. Ducks are cooked in similar fashion. Another flavorful method of preparing duck, or chicken, is to heavily coat the bird with a pounded paste of chilies, turmeric, and garlic. Wrapped in a well-secured banana leaf, it is barbecued over slow-burning charcoal. Food on Bali is very hot and spicy. Fruits, vegetables, grains, fish, and shellfish are abundant here. The soil is amazingly fertile, the climate one of perpetual summer, and the people a delight. Meticulously sculpted terraced rice paddies, alternately green, gold, and black, cover the mountain slopes. The paddies are emerald-colored while the shoots grow, golden when the rice is ripe, and black when the farmer burns off the stalks. Three rice harvests a year are common now with the new cultivating techniques. Powdery white beaches, spectacular sunsets, and a happy smiling people who devote their energies to art and religion have all contributed to make this island a paradise on earth.

The terrain of Irian Jaya and the Mollucas is not suitable for rice cultivation. Staple foods are sago palm flour, cassava root, and sometimes plantains. Sago flour is made from the pith centered in the trunk of a sago palm tree. Washed and dried, the pith is ground into flour. The simplest method of baking sago flour bread is to leave it to bake in the sun until it is dense and hard. It can also be made in a clay mold with depressions to hold the dough—a bit like our corn pone molds. The mold is heated until it reaches red heat, the dough is pushed into the depressions, topped with a banana leaf and something to weigh it down, and is left baking in the residual heat of the mold. Either way sago flour bread does not have a great deal of flavor, and the bread has to be dipped in water to soften before eating. Cassava root, eaten as a vegetable when young and tender, is ground into flour when mature. Cassava leaves are a good source of vitamin C, and, cooked in coconut milk, are eaten throughout the islands. Compared to the spicy cooking of the rest of the archipelago, the dishes here may seem bland. Sweet and sour tastes predominate, chili peppers are used sparingly, and the most distinctive flavors come from the use of abundant local herbs. Irian Jaya tribal people enjoy a meal of python when they can find one. In Jayapura, Indonesian dishes are accessible in most restaurants, and a few serve European and Chinese food.

Chinese, Arabs, Indians, Spanish, Portuguese, English, and Dutch have all left their imprint on the language, culture, and cooking of Indonesia. Curries, cumin, coriander, and caraway were introduced from India; dill and fennel from the Middle East; peanuts, pineapple, papaya, coffee, and many temperate vegetables from Europe. Chili peppers came by way of Mexico. China contributed black pepper, cinnamon, and the indispensable wok which is in daily use throughout the islands. Indonesia's ability to assimilate all these foreign influences, plus their own masterful blending of local spices and herbs, make Indonesian cuisine one of the most flavorful and creative in the world. Some of the many seasonings in daily use are nutmeg, star anise, mace, cinnamon, cardamom, cumin, caraway, lemongrass, sesame seeds, *trassi* (fermented shrimp paste), soy sauce, and *kecap manis*, a sauce made with soy sauce, sugar, garlic, and ginger. Coconuts are used in hundreds of dishes. The delectable, tender flesh of a very young coconut is eaten with a spoon directly from the shell. Grated meat of the mature nut is used in dishes both savory and sweet, and, as a garnish, plain or toasted. Recipes are plentiful for fish, poultry, vegetables, and meats cooked in coconut milk in both Indonesia and Malaysia—dessert recipes usually call for an extra dollop of coconut cream. Coconut cream comes from the first squeezing of freshly grated coconut. Coconut milk is from the second squeezing, after a little water has been added. It is astonishing how rich, thick, and creamy sauces made with coconut cream can be. Their smoothness belies the absence of butter and eggs.

The coconut palm is called the "Tree of Life" by many Pacific island cultures. From its roots to its fernlike leaves, it provides food, drink, tools, shelter, and herbal medicines. There are 36 species of coconut palm. The liquid inside a coconut is nutritious, thirst-quenching, and has "cooling" properties. Fresh coconut meat yields protein, lipids, carbohydrates, calcium, and other valuable minerals. Copra, dried coconut meat, is processed into coconut oil, which in turn is used to make cooking oil, margarine, soap, candles, and perfume. The copra residue is used as animal feed. Delicious vegetarian dishes are made from the heart of the coconut palm, and from its tender young leaves. The sap extracted from palm flower buds is boiled down to make palm sugar. Palm sugar naturally ferments into a delightful toddy. When distilled, this fermented juice becomes arrack—a potent alcoholic brew. Soured, it makes a hearty vinegar. The roots of the palm generate a soothing gargle for sore throats, and a medicine that alleviates dysentery. All Southeast Asian kitchens have ladles and cups fashioned from coconut shells. The thick fibrous husk around the shell is used as a mattress stuffing and made into string. The leaves furnish baskets, hats, matting, and thatch for roofs. The strong middle spine of the leaf is turned into brooms, poles, and firewood. The "Tree of Life" is aptly named.

Meat, poultry, and fish are often marinated in spice mixtures to tenderize and to add flavor. After the food is cooked, the remaining marinade, napped with coconut milk, provides a delightful sauce. *Satay*, shrimp or strips of meat or chicken threaded on a bamboo skewer and grilled, is enormously popular everywhere, either as an appetizer, a snack, or a main dish. *Satay* is commonly dipped in a spicy peanut sauce or in *kecap manis* (a sweetened soy-based sauce). The bamboo skewers are soaked in cold water for an hour or so before grilling to delay conflagration. *Satay* sellers roam the streets of Indonesia, carrying their kitchens on their backs. It takes but a minute to set down the charcoal brazier, fan the coals, and cook to order.

Eating in the streets is a way of life in Indonesia. Dozens of *warungs*—wheeled, makeshift food stalls—appear on street corners at mealtimes, in every town and village, selling very good, freshly cooked foods, snacks, and drinks. They cluster near food markets, office buildings at noon time, and in village squares. The cooking is delicious, plentiful, and cheap. People patronize more than one *warung* at a time, taking this delicacy from one, that from another. Seating can be on benches, stools, or simply on a rug set down by the *warung* owner. *Warungs* that sell just coffee are for men only. They are a big part of village life, where men meet to socialize or to read the news, especially in the evenings.

Dishes such as *nasi goreng* (fried rice) or *mie goreng* (fried noodles), *cap cai* (chop suey), *gado gado* (cooked vegetable salad with peanut sauce), and various curries of beef, lamb, or chicken, *krupuk*, fried *tempe*, *satays*, and *martabak* (a savory filled Arab pancake), *pisang goreng* (fried bananas) and, of course, *sambal*, are staple fare. *Ronde*—a ginger syrup drink with hot water, fruit, and balls of sticky rice, is traditional, as is *tuak*—rice beer—and hot or spiced tea.

Bounty from the Sea

As one would expect of a country with thousands of miles of coastline, and oceans teeming with innumerable varieties of fish and shellfish, seafood is an integral part of the Indonesian diet. Fish soups, using every part of the fish to maximize the flavor, are delicious. To prevent the thick savory concoction from sticking to the pan, small potatoes are used to line the bottom of the pot. Fish and shrimp are often grilled with a spicy topping, baked in coconut milk or wrapped in a banana leaf and steamed. Large, shiny, fragrant banana leaves are wrapped around whole fish and chickens, as well as small mixtures of food, before cooking over charcoal. This not only minimizes moisture loss over the hot coals, but imparts a delicate flavor and aroma from the wrapping to the finished dish. The packet, slit open at the table, looks both intriguing and appetizing. In some modern kitchens, the cooks go one better and cover the banana leaf in aluminum foil to prevent loss of flavor from the leaf! Banana leaves double for plates when none are at hand. A beautiful dish is the slender stalk of a young banana palm, hollowed out, stuffed with a savory rice mixture and baked. If very tender, the stalk is sliced, gently cooked in coconut milk, and spiced with fiery chili peppers. The banana trunk consists of tightly overlapping leaf sheaths. The plant produces a big reddish-purple bud that also is used in cooking.

Shrimp are so plentiful that often a handful is tossed into a vegetable dish for added color and texture. Shrimp fritters are sold everywhere. Sulawesi natives serve them with butter or Chinese sweet-and-sour sauce. Meat is scarce and eaten mainly in urban areas. Unless imported, it is often of poor quality. For the farmer it is more important to keep cattle for tilling the land, or for producing milk, than to slaughter it for the table. Poultry is plentiful. Goat herds flourish for the benefit of the nonpork-eating Muslims, as do herds of pigs for the Buddhists, Hindus, Chinese, and Christians. The soybean is very important to the health and well-being of the rural people of Indonesia. Tofu (soybean cakes) and tempe (a fermented soy product), usually sold wrapped in a banana leaf, are the chief sources of protein for many people living inland. Soy sauce is used in savory dishes throughout the archipelago. Pickled foods, similar to the *acar* of Malaysia, are a part of most meals.

Rice, called *nasi*, is the chief staple of Indonesia. Several crops are grown each year in thousands upon thousands of flooded rice paddies, on terraced hills in mountainous regions, and on slash-and-burn tracts in the jungles. A common practice, learned from the

Japanese, is to slip young fish into the flooded rice paddy to mature alongside the rice shoots.

Rice is served steaming hot, in a basket, in copious amounts at every meal. Served with fiery *sambal*, it is called *nasi champur*. Indonesians prefer their rice to be as white and fluffy as possible, with the unfortunate consequence that a great deal of the nutritious hull is lost in the polishing process. For breakfast, rice is sometimes topped with an egg, or fried—*nasi goreng*—and garnished with minced fried shallots, chilies, and soy sauce. Lunch is quite often a substantial meal, and may include a sauced dish of chicken or meat, barbecued *satay* or grilled fish, a salad of boiled vegetables accompanied by a peanut *sambal* and *krupuk* (rice crackers). Delicate-tasting, hot soup is always served at meals and is meant to be sipped between mouthfuls. Small and varied dishes of hot, crunchy, highly spiced *sambals* are placed within easy reach. The freshest of luscious fruits finish the meal, followed perhaps by ginger tea or coffee. Dinner would be basically the same but with more dishes—perhaps two or more vegetable dishes and an additional fish curry. Sometimes families will go

Rice plant with grain

out later in the evening to have dessert at a favorite foodstall. Alcohol is forbidden to Muslims, and it is rarely served at meals. However, the Hindu Balinese have a good time on occasion with their pale pink rice liquor, called Brem. A working man's tipple is coconut toddy.

Indonesian food has a reputation for being too hot for Western palates. Their spicy sauces were created to be eaten sparingly, with large quantities of rice, and not, as we do, with the emphasis on the dish and only a side serving of rice. This makes a great deal of difference. Some households and restaurants serve the hottest jolt in their small dishes of *sambal*. This method allows each person to mix into his food his preferred ratio of heat to rice. Fresh chilies, crystallized with sugar, are readily accessible for those who lust after chili's searing bite for dessert. Sweet desserts and candies, which the Indonesians love, are also made with rice: rice and palm sugar cooked in banana leaves, sweet cakes flavored with coconut or fruits, intensely sweetened rice puddings topped with thick coconut cream, or sweet sticky rice topped with grated coconuts or sliced ripe mangoes. One spectacular dessert is a seeded pumpkin shell filled with a luscious melange of beaten eggs, palm sugar, and coconut cream, gently steamed until the custard sets.

Rice flour is made into hundreds of different products: from noodles and rice cakes to the ubiquitous, highly colored, rice flour cracker called *krupuk*. Flavored with flaked fish, shellfish, shrimp paste, or sweetened with fruit—particularly dried bananas—nutritious *krupuk*, when dropped in hot fat, puffs up and curves into a ladle-shaped cracker. Consumed as a snack, it also doubles as a scoop when eating, as we use potato chips with dips. *Krupuk* makes a handy substitute for bread, which is not generally a part of Indonesian cooking except on the eastern edge of the archipelago where the terrain is not conducive to rice-growing.

Indonesia, astride the equator with an often wet and always hot climate, produces a staggering abundance of fruits and vegetables, many of which are found nowhere else. A number of tropical vegetables we enjoy here in America are imported from Southeast Asia. Among these are: tiny round eggplants, no larger than an orange, either pale green or striped green and white; pea eggplants, marble-sized and bitter, used in soups; Chinese yard-long beans which, though longer than ours, taste the same; water spinach (*Kankung*), an aquatic leaf with a taste similar to spinach; icicle radish, about 7 inches long and pure white; various fungi such as cloud ears, tree ears, and straw mushrooms; different kinds of gourds, including bitter melon, also called Balsam pear or apple—this has a long ridged shape about the size of a cucumber, and its bitter taste can be ameliorated by slicing and soaking it in salted water—and tamarind, the sour-tasting fruit surrounding the seed of the feathery-leaved tamarind tree. In addition to vegetables, Indonesian cooks routinely throw chunks of ripe, juicy fruit into their curries, salads, and stir-fries. Fried unripe bananas are a delicious, savory side dish. The purple-skinned *mangosteen*, which grows wild in the jungles of Kalimantan, is prized for its white, sour/sweet juicy flesh. *Salak* is another sourish fruit with a snake-patterned skin. *Pomelos*, a fruit similar to grapefruit, are from the citrus family, as are Indonesia's enormous quantities of limes, lemons, oranges, and tangerines. *Jambu air*, the rose apple, is a small, juicy, bell-shaped fruit often eaten with a dipping sauce of soy, sugar, and red chili peppers. Passion fruit, filled with black seeds amid a rich, golden pulp, has a glorious taste, as do luscious tree-ripened guavas, papayas, mangoes, and over forty varieties of banana, ranging in color from cream to red, and in size from finger-length to the enormous *pisang rajah*, which reaches a yard in length. Jack fruit is another huge fruit weighing in at 60–70 pounds. Its large seeds are surrounded by great-tasting, golden flesh. Occasionally for dessert, fruit is marinated in an unexpected mixture of vinegar, sugar, and chilies, and sometimes steamed bananas are teamed with a lightly spiced syrup, but fresh fruit is the rule. Fruit juice is popular at meals, as is coconut milk sweetened with palm sugar, palm wine, and an avocado drink called *es pokat*.

Many Indonesian dishes are ideal for entertaining. Well suited to advance preparation and refrigeration are dishes wrapped in leaves or foil; spiced rice dishes that need only last-minute additions of meat, fish, chicken, and vegetables; and *satays*, marinated and skewered in advance. These can all be reheated or quickly grilled just before serving. *Sambal*, the ubiquitous highly spiced chili sauce, for which there are an infinite number of recipes, can be made ahead, covered tightly, and stored in the refrigerator for days. Do-ahead sauces made with coconut milk are best kept in the freezer.

Indonesian poultry is often parboiled in sauce or stock—as it can be somewhat sinewy—then refrigerated, to be later coated with

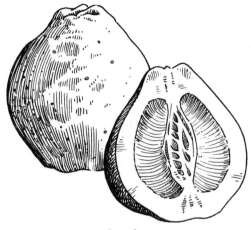

Pomelo

spices prior to grilling. Minced shallots or onions, fried until dark brown and crisp, are frequently sprinkled over Indonesian dishes, as is spicy, stir-fried, grated coconut. Both of these garnishes can be made in batches and kept in tightly closed glass jars in the refrigerator until needed. Salads of cooked, chilled vegetables, sometimes garnished with raw tomato, cucumber, or cilantro, often appear accompanied by a cooked, thick, spicy dressing made with coconut milk or ground peanuts which is reheated at the last minute. This famous dish, served in slightly different ways all over Indonesia, is called *gado gado*. Cold, cooked dressings are thickened with mashed hard-cooked egg yolks, or even mashed potatoes. The spices, vinegar, or citrus juices are then beaten in until the desired consistency is reached. Freshly grated coconut is a component of salads, a garnish, and an ingredient in the dressing. Cooked rice or noodle salads, combined with seafood, vegetables, and fruits, appear frequently with a cooked coconut milk dressing. All these ingredients may be readied ahead of time and combined at the last minute. These delicious dressings owe their flavor to tamarind, ginger, crushed peanuts, turmeric, soy sauce, or citrus juices, rather than the fiery chili pepper. Turmeric root, both fresh, dried, and ground, flavors foods throughout Southeast Asia. Young turmeric leaves add great flavor to soups. Curries are particularly suited to advance preparation: their complex flavors mellow and improve with keeping.

Reproducing these unusual and elegant foods in your own kitchens will not be difficult. The average Indonesian kitchen is equipped with large and small mortars and pestles, a heavy grinding stone for roots and spices, colanders, sieves, sharp knives, a sharp cleaver, and a hefty chopping block. Most tasks may be taken care of in an American kitchen with a food processor.

Recipes from Indonesia

Steamed Bass in Spiced Nut Sauce

1½	lb.	bass, cleaned
6		candle nuts or 9 macadamia nuts
2		quarter-sized slices of fresh ginger
½	t.	salt
1		seeded plum tomato, sliced
4	tiny	hot red chilies, seeded
5		shallots
2		scallions
½	small	red onion
1	T.	peanut oil
		aluminum foil to make 14-inch square

In a food processor, chop the nuts coarsely, then add the ginger, salt, tomato slices, chilies, shallots, scallions, and red onion. Whirl to make a paste, then stir in the peanut oil.

Place one-third of this mixture in the middle of the aluminum square, place fish on top of the paste, and place another one-third of the paste in the cavity of the fish. Scrape remaining paste over fish and fold to make a secure package.

Place package over boiling water in a large steamer and steam, covered, for 30 minutes. Replenish water from time to time, if necessary.   *Serves 4*

Kalimantan Shrimp

1	T.	tamarind paste
1		shallot, sliced

1	garlic clove
3	red chilies, seeded and sliced
	½-inch piece fresh ginger, sliced
1 t.	salt
2 t.	brown sugar
2	Italian tomatoes, seeded and diced
2 T.	peanut oil
2 lb.	shrimp, peeled and deveined
	lime wedges

Soak the tamarind paste for 10 minutes in a quarter cup of warm water. Strain, discarding solids. Pour into a food processor and add the shallot, garlic, chilies, ginger, salt, sugar, and tomato. Whirl to a paste. Heat half of the oil in a wok and stir-fry the paste for 3 or 4 minutes over medium heat. Set aside. In a skillet, stir-fry the shrimp over high heat, using the remaining oil, for 2 minutes. Transfer shrimp to the wok and stir-fry, coating well with the paste, for another minute or two.

Serve with the lime wedges. *Serves 6*

Corn Fritters

2	shallots, sliced
1	garlic clove, chopped
1 T.	cilantro, chopped
1½ C.	fresh corn kernels
1	egg
½ C.	flour
¼ t.	baking powder
½ t.	freshly ground cumin
¾ t.	sea salt
¼ C.	corn oil for frying

In a food processor, make a paste with the onion, garlic, and cilantro. Add the corn and process very briefly just to soften kernels a little. Beat the egg lightly and add to the corn mixture. Sift the flour, baking powder, ground cumin, and salt into a bowl, add the corn mixture and stir thoroughly. If mixture is very thick, stir in one tablespoon of water at a time until mixture reaches a batter consistency. Heat oil in a large skillet, or electric fry pan at 360°F. Using a quarter-cup measure, carefully pour batter into pan, frying until light brown on both sides. Serve hot with a *sambal*, or serve as a side dish.

Makes about 10 fritters

Vegetable, Egg, and Noodle Salad

½ C.	raw peanuts
4	eggs, hard-boiled and quartered
2 C.	bean sprouts
1 C.	snow peas
¼ lb.	Chinese egg noodles or linguine
1 T.	tamarind paste
½ t.	salt
1 T.	brown sugar
1 T.	fresh lime juice
2	garlic cloves, sliced
2 small	red chilies, seeded and sliced
½ C.	seeded cucumber, cubed
1 C.	shredded Chinese or Napa cabbage
1 C.	cooked boiling potatoes, cubed
2 T.	lightly chopped fresh cilantro

Roast the raw peanuts for 10 minutes, in a moderately hot oven. Cool and rub off the skins. Meanwhile, hard-boil and quarter the eggs, refrigerate. Blanch the bean sprouts and snow peas in boiling water for 1 minute. Drain and refrigerate. Cook the Chinese noodles or linguine until tender but still fairly firm. Drain and set aside. Soak the tamarind paste in a quarter-cup of warm water for 10 minutes, strain, and discard solids. Chop peanuts coarsely. In a food processor, make a paste with the tamarind liquid, salt, sugar, lime juice, garlic, and chilies. Toss all the vegetables and noodles with the paste. Garnish with the eggs and cilantro and serve at room temperature.

Serves 6–8

Roast Chicken with Spices and Coconut Milk

5–6 lb.	roasting chicken
2	garlic cloves

1	medium	onion, chopped
2	fresh	hot red chilies
1	t.	tamarind paste
½	t.	shrimp paste, dried OR
½	t.	anchovy paste
2	T.	dark soy sauce
1	T.	fresh lime juice
½	t.	ground black pepper
¼	t.	salt
½	C.	coconut milk
		fresh coriander leaves for garnish

Wash chicken and pat dry with paper towels. In a blender or mini food processor, make a paste with the garlic, onion, chilies, tamarind paste, shrimp or anchovy paste, soy sauce, lime juice, pepper, and salt. Rub this paste all over the chicken inside and out. Marinate chicken in a shallow dish for 2 hours. Heat the coconut milk in a wok and cook chicken, breast side down, over medium-low heat for 25 minutes, scraping all the remaining marinade from the dish onto the chicken. Baste with sauce occasionally. Carefully turn chicken over and cook for an additional 30 minutes. Meanwhile, preheat oven to 375°F. Place chicken breast side down on a rack in a roasting pan, pour sauce over chicken. Rinse wok with half a cup of water and pour into roasting pan. Roast chicken for 30 minutes. Turn chicken breast side up and roast for 20–25 minutes or until juice runs clear when pricked with a fork. Remove from oven to serving plate. Garnish with coriander leaves. Degrease sauce and serve separately. *Serves 3–4*

Sambal—Hot and Spicy

8	fresh	red chilies, seeded and sliced
8		candlenuts or 10 Macadamia nuts
½	t.	salt
		juice of 1 lemon
1–2	T.	chicken broth, if needed

Using a mini food processor, or a blender, process the chilies, nuts, salt, and lemon juice to a smooth paste, adding drops of chicken broth to facilitate processing, if needed.

Chicken Satay

1 lb.	boneless chicken breast, cut into 1½-inch cubes

Marinade

	small star anise
3	garlic cloves
3 T.	tamarind paste, diluted in ¼ C. water and strained
1	thin small slice fresh ginger
1 T.	soy sauce
½ t.	brown sugar
½ T.	fresh ground black pepper
½ t.	sea salt
2 T.	peanut oil
8	wooden skewers, soaked for 30 minutes in water

Peanut sauce

⅓–½ C.	peanut butter
2 large	garlic cloves
2 small	fresh red chili peppers, seeded and minced
2 t.	fresh lemon juice
2 t.	brown sugar
½ T.	fresh ginger, minced
1 T.	soy sauce
½ C.	hot water

Place chicken cubes in a medium-sized bowl and toss in the star anise. Using a food processor, whirl the remaining marinade ingredients and pour over the chicken cubes, mixing to distribute the marinade evenly. Refrigerate for about 1 hour. Meanwhile, using a food processor, blend the peanut sauce ingredients, and set aside.

Remove the chicken cubes from the marinade, discarding the star anise, and thread them evenly on the soaked wooden skewers. Brush with peanut oil and broil over coals, or under the broiler, for 5 minutes or until cooked through. Serve with the peanut sauce.

Serves 8 as an appetizer

Savory Rice with Spiced Scallops and Cremini Mushrooms

4	T.	sesame oil
l	lb.	sea scallops, sliced crosswise if large
½	t.	sea salt
⅓	C.	minced red onion
l	t.	paprika
2	T.	tomato sauce, preferably homemade
2	T.	tamari sauce
l	t.	brown sugar
4	C.	cooked white rice
3		garlic cloves, minced
		1" x 1" piece fresh ginger, shredded
l	large	onion, sliced thinly
2	T.	fresh coriander, minced
2–3		fresh red chilies, seeded and minced (wear rubber gloves)
l	t.	shrimp paste
2	t.	grated lime zest
½	t.	freshly ground cumin
⅓	lb.	fresh cremini mushrooms, well-washed and halved
¼	C.	thinly sliced scallions
½		thin, seedless cucumber, sliced OR fresh watercress sprigs for garnish

Toss sea scallops with sea salt, set aside for 1 minute, then rinse and pat dry. Heat half of the oil in a wok over medium heat, and stir-fry the minced red onion for 30 seconds. Stir in paprika, tomato sauce, soy sauce, and brown sugar and cook for 2 to 3 minutes to soften onion. Add cooked rice and toss until hot and evenly coated with sauce. Arrange rice in a ring on a shallow, heatproof dish, and keep warm in a low oven.

Heat remaining oil in wok, and stir-fry garlic, ginger, and onion for 1 minute over medium heat. Add coriander, chilies, shrimp paste, lemon zest, and cumin to wok and cook until fragrant. Stir in cremini mushrooms, lower heat, and continue stir-frying until mushrooms are cooked, about 5 minutes. Increase heat, add sea scallops, and stir-fry for 2 to 3 minutes, or until scallops are opaque. Remove dish from oven, and spoon scallop mixture into the center of the rice circle.

Arrange cucumber slices or watercress sprigs around edge of dish and sprinkle with minced scallions.   *Serves 4*

Indonesian Baked Banana Pudding

4		eggs
1	C.	brown sugar
1		12 oz. can of coconut milk
2	t.	vanilla
3		ripe bananas
		pinch of salt

Preheat oven to 350°F. In a large bowl, beat the eggs with an electric mixer until light colored. Gradually beat in the sugar and the coconut milk a little at a time. Whisk in the vanilla. Slice bananas about ½-inch thick and fold into batter. Pour pudding into a deep, well-buttered soufflé dish, and place dish in a pan with enough hot water to come 2 inches up the side of the soufflé dish. Bake for 45–50 minutes, or until a tester comes out clean. Cool and refrigerate until serving.

Serves 6

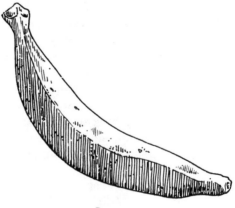

Banana

THE PHILIPPINES

The cooking of the Philippines is quite different from any other
country in Southeast Asia. Ingredients such as cheese and tomato sauce are used here and nowhere else. Everyday dishes are
closer to the cooking of Spain than to their own native food. Spanish
colonization of the Philippines lasted for almost 400 years
(1521–1898), and because of this long association, Filipinos consider
Spanish fare as much their own as any local dish in their repertoire.
Probably 30 percent of Filipino recipes are of Spanish origin. The two
prevailing techniques learned from the Spanish are sautéing and
stewing (or braising). Garlic and onions sautéd in olive oil or lard—
the first step in many recipes—gives a taste to Filipino food that is
unique. Annatto seeds, *achuete*, which give a red color to food, were
introduced from Mexico, as were many vegetables, including corn,
avocado, and coffee beans. Gradually, Filipino cooks added Spanish
ingredients to their Malay and Chinese foods, and more often than
not gave the dish a Spanish name. To the Filipinos Spain symbolized
elegance, and because of this Spanish dishes were always served in
upperclass society, when entertaining in Manila.

Spanish culinary techniques and foods are all-pervasive, greatly
diminishing all other foreign influences. Spain, Portugal, and Mexico
inspired such dishes as *empanadas*, meat-filled pastries; *morcon*, rolled
flank steak stuffed with sausage and hard-boiled eggs; *pochero*, a slow-
cooking mixture of meats, sausage, sweet potatoes, tomatoes, *saba* bananas (plantains), chick peas and other vegetables, which dissolve into

a thick savory sauce; *bacalhao,* dried salt cod from Portugal, an ingredient used in fish balls and fritters; *caldereta,* a goat stew—the same name is given to a fish dish of Spanish origin; several different kinds of *arroz à la paella; menudo,* a stew made with pork, pork liver, tomatoes, and potatoes, flavored with annatto seeds; chicken *relleno,* a fiesta dish of chicken stuffed with pork, boiled eggs, sausage, and spices; *chorizo de Bilbao,* a strongly flavored sausage, eaten with enthusiasm in both Spain and Portugal, and a milder sausage that Filipinos eat for breakfast sometimes topped with an egg; *adobo,* from Mexico, a rich stew simmered in vinegar, garlic, and pepper, which has become the Philippines' national dish; sweet desserts include *leche flan,* a creamy custard often topped with sweetened soft young coconut, called *macapuno;* and *membrillo,* a thinly sliced candy made from cooked guava paste.

Compared to Vietnamese or Thai food, suffused as it is with scorching hot chilies, native Filipino food seems very mild, almost bland, on first acquaintance. But further investigation reveals assertive sour, salty, bitter, and sweet tastes that define Filipino cuisine. Sour flavors predominate. One of the best-loved of these is a small

Philippine woven basket shape

limelike citrus fruit, called *kalamansi*, which is spritzed generously over food at the table, particularly noodle dishes. Filipinos are also partial to the tart, unripened, fruit pulp and the leaves of tamarind, which is squirted into the pot during cooking. Other green, sour fruits used in the same way are immature guava, pineapple, green mango, and *kamias*, an astringent cucumber-shaped fruit. Prior to cooking, meats and fish are routinely marinated in palm vinegar. Palm vinegar is half as strong, and acidic, as our regular vinegar. This practice was started to preserve food's freshness, before everybody had refrigeration. It continues because the Filipinos have grown to love sour tastes and would not give them up at any price. Sour-tasting dishes can be remarkably restorative on a hot, sultry day. Bowls of pickled foods, called *achar*, similar to the *acar* of Malaysia and Indonesia, are placed on the table at each meal, as is an array of strongly flavored condiments and relishes. It is expected in Filipino homes and in restaurants that everybody will want to season their food themselves, and a jar of *bagoong*, fermented fish, a bottle of *patis*, fermented fish sauce, a dish of vinegar spiked with chili, and peppery vegetable relishes are provided for this purpose. They are used as ubiquitously as we use salt and pepper.

One of the biggest archipelagos in the world, the Philippines encompasses 7,107 islands and islets—less than 5,000 of which are named, and only 1,000 or so inhabited. Strategically placed between Taiwan to the north and Borneo to the south, the archipelago sits astride travel lanes that connect the South China Sea and the Pacific Ocean. The Philippines is approximately the size of the state of Arizona. The three main island groups are Luzon, Mindanao, and the Visayas. Over 90 percent of Filipinos live on the two largest islands, Luzon and Mindanao, which encompass two-thirds of the land mass. One of the deepest seas in the world, called the Philippine Deep, is located off the island of Mindoro, which is separated from Luzon by the narrow, boat-filled Verde Island Passage. Rugged mountains, fertile valleys, and extensive river systems crisscross the bigger islands. These "Rios Grandes" serve as waterways for mid-sized ocean vessels and for native crafts. Steaming rain forests, partially unexplored, are inhabited by formerly head-hunting tribesmen. Over a thousand varieties of orchid grow in the rain forests, some with blossoms measuring five inches across. It is said that the most beautiful flowers bloom high in the canopy close to the light and are rarely seen. Fifty-four known varieties of bamboo grow profusely throughout the islands. Bamboo has myriad uses, from making musical instruments and hats, to housing construction and bridge building. Many of the taller mountains are volcanic in origin. The turbulent land of the Philippines suffers numerous typhoons and volcanic eruptions. These explosions often spawn in their wake considerable earthquake activity. The colossal eruption of Mount Pinatuba, on June 15, 1991, located 55 miles (88.5 kilometers) northwest of Manila, spewed 2 cubic miles (3.2 cubic kilometers) of superheated ash into the atmosphere, darkening downtown Manila in mid-afternoon. The ash formed a cloud that gradually girdled the earth, blocking 2 percent of the sunlight, and slightly lowering the world's temperature.

The Philippine islands are incredibly beautiful. Bordered as they are with pristine beaches, and water so clear that you can see the pattern made by the tide in the sand beneath you as you swim. Coconut palms shelter the small, thatched houses, called *nipa* huts, their gardens awash with bougainvillea and hibiscus. Many of the islands are ringed with coral reefs.

The Chinese have been sailing to the Philippine islands to trade silk, ivory, and porcelain for native products, since the seventh century. During the eleventh and twelfth centuries, they set up trading posts, married Filipinas, and made the islands their home. The Chinese shared with the Filipinos their knowledge of mining and metal work, showed them how useful umbrellas could be in a country with such frequent rain showers, and taught them the joy of deafening one another with gongs and gunpowder. Trade between the two nations at that time was by bartering. Also in the 1300s, Arab and Indian Muslims settled in the islands to proselytize their Islamic faith. Islam spread northward from Borneo to the southern Philippine islands. India's contribution to the Philippines was mainly in the arts, curry spices, and the Hindu religion.

Hominid remains dating back 30,000 years, found on Palawan, an archipelago of 2,000 unexplored islets in the southwestern part of the Philippines, suggest that early man came across land bridges that connected the islands to China and Borneo. The species of wildlife found in the rain forests of Palawan, Mindanao, and Sulu are closely related to the wildlife on Borneo, and wildlife on Luzon is very similar to that of Taiwan and China, confirming that land bridges did indeed exist. Chinese, Arabs, and Indians mention the islands in their historical literature, but their accounts are sometimes contradictory. The first recorded history of the Philippines began in 1521, with the arrival of Ferdinand Magellan, the brave Spanish explorer, who discovered the archipelago and claimed the land for Spain. His horrendous two-year voyage was plagued by disease and near starvation. King Philip II, for whom the archipelago is named, was adamant that the Philippines should be subdued without the appalling loss of life that had occurred during the Spanish conquest of New Spain (now Mexico). This restraint worked in his favor, and within ten years the conquest was complete.

The Cuisine of the Philippines

Filipino cuisine reflects the culinary influences of the Spanish, the Malays, and the Chinese who came as settlers, traders, immigrants, or conquerors, and chose to live on the islands. Arabs and Indian Muslims also came to trade, carrying their favorite spices—cumin and coriander. The Chinese introduced bean curds and noodles to the Philippines. Egg rolls, soy sauce, and a taste for cooked vegetable dishes such as *Guisadong Sitaw*, sautéd green beans, all hail from China. They traded their beautiful porcelain jars, silk, ivory, and metals for pearls, gold, coral, and amber, and also honey, sea cucumbers, and shark fins for soups. Chinese noodle dishes, *pancit*, are found throughout the Philippines, each with a different sauce made from local ingredients. A particular favorite is *pancit luglug*, for which the sauce includes shrimps or shrimp sauce and peppers fried in garlic, patis, and sour lime juice, with a sprinkling of pork crackling and chopped boiled egg. Two immensely popular noodles are *sotanghon*, bean threads, and *bihon*, rice sticks. Egg rolls have evolved into *lumpia*, a thin sheet of noodle dough rolled around a savory filling. A multiplicity of different stuffings fill these delicious appetizers—shrimp, pork, garlic, and various seasonings. They can be fried and served hot (*Lumpia Shanghai*) with a sauce of cooked vinegar, soy sauce, crushed garlic, black pepper, and tomato. A typically Filipino method is to line the wrapping with fresh salad leaves and fill them with freshly cooked ingredients, such as lobster or shrimp, mixed with julienned hearts of palm, and serve them cold (*Lumpia Ubod*) with a precooked sauce of vinegar, garlic, and brown sugar. Some Asian markets in America carry prepared *lumpia* in jars. More recent Malay settlers brought their knowledge of hot chilies and the use of coconut milk. The cooking of the Malays in the south closely resembles the fiery cuisine of their forebears on the island of Sumatra. Hot chilies spice their dishes and coconut enriches and smooths their sauces. All Filipino dishes with *ginataang* (coconut milk) in them are part of the Malaysian heritage, as are goat and lamb dishes spiked with hot chilies. The American influence is seen in the Filipinos' fondness for steak, hamburgers, apple pie, and canned soft drinks. Some canned American foods are used for convenience, for example, evaporated milk in place of water buffalo milk for custards. Salads, laced with mayonnaise, and sandwiches were brought to the Philippines by the Americans. American salads, particularly chicken salad and potato salad, are always part of the menu on special occasions.

The Spanish took Manila, as their colonial capital, on Luzon island, at Manila Bay—one of widest natural harbors in the world. Shipping is protected there from typhoons by the surrounding mountains. Luzon and the Visayas were quickly colonized. However, Muslim-dominated islands far to the south, and the mostly animist hilltribes in inaccessible mountain areas, were never completely subdued. Their customs, rituals, and religious affiliations remain intact to this day. Despite this the Spanish achieved a governable whole from over 7,000 far-flung islands, and ruled for over three hundred years from the small, walled city in Manila. By the mid 1500s, Islam had started to spread northward and the archipelago would undoubtedly have become an Islamic nation but for the staunchly Roman Catholic Spanish colonists. Following on the heels of the Spanish soldiers, came Spanish friars who successfully converted their separate regions to Roman Catholicism. Today the vast majority of Filipinos are devout Roman Catholics. Catholicism helped unify the islanders, many of whom soon learned to speak Spanish. Spanish music, art, and dance were also unifying factors. The Spanish fandango, along with native dances, is performed today with gusto at all native fiestas.

During the years 1575 to 1815, the Spanish expanded trade between the Philippines and other Asian countries, shipping to Acapulco, twice yearly, oriental goods such as perfume, ivory, silk, tea, and spices, and returning to Manila loaded with silver from New Spain. Native industries were neglected, as investment in the galleon trade proved more profitable. With Mexico's independence, Spain's trade monopolies ceased. Open trade created a new class of wealthy Filipinos whose children, educated in Europe, came home with democratic principles that spawned nationalism. Discontent was fomented by the novels of Dr. José Rizal whose books called upon the colonial government to implement peaceful reform. José Rizal, a national hero, was executed in 1896. Armed revolt continued to escalate. In 1898, following the Spanish American War, Spain sold the Philippines to the United States. The American colonists stayed for almost 50 years. In 1940, with the first president, Manual Quezon, in office, the Japanese attacked Luzon, delaying independence for the Filipinos until 1946. The American colonization, though brief, was instrumental in raising the Filipino standard of living, through public health programs and improved sanitation methods, and free elementary education. Classes, taught in English, gave the Filipinos a common language. Filipinos accommodate to change easily, and they have the most Western outlook of any Southeast Asian country.

The people of the Philippines were originally of Malay stock. Intermarriage with traders, immigrants, and conquerors over the years has resulted in mestizos. These people of mixed Malay, Chinese, and Spanish blood gave the islands their own distinct cultural identity and fostered a desire to govern themselves. Today the Philippines has a population of over 61 million, more than half of whom average less than eighteen years of age. With so many young people ready to enter the work force each year, finding jobs is difficult. In lowland areas, the overwhelming majority of workers are engaged in fishing, farming, and forestry. Over 70 percent of the population inhabit flat coastal areas, and Luzon's huge rice-growing Central Plain near Manila Bay. However, the population on the islands of Mindanao, Palawan, and Mindoro is gradually increasing as people flee their cramped living conditions in densely packed rural areas.

Filipinos raise their children to be gentle, polite, and very religious. Girls are given more chores to do than boys even when they are quite young, and more is expected of them throughout their lives.

Young women stay in school longer. Almost all of the doctorates, and three-quarters of the masters degrees are earned by women. The majority of dentists, pharmacists, and teachers are women, and, increasingly, they are making their presence felt in banking, medicine, and law. It is not uncommon for women to support their husbands and children. Yet Filipinas, renowned for their grace and femininity, are not particularly feminist. It is simply that families are close-knit, divorce is illegal, and looking after one another is expected of all family members. The elderly are respected and well-cared for. For a Filipino, putting elderly parents in a home for the aged is unthinkable. Gentle and generous, Filipinos are also very hospitable people. Food is synonymous with good will, and it's almost impossible to have a 5-minute conversation with a Filipino without being invited to share a meal. Anyone who visits a Filipino home, at whatever time of day, is immediately offered food. An invitation to join an ongoing meal is extended at once, and a refusal would not be taken well. Cakes, sweet snacks, and other delicacies are offered if no meal is in progress, which is unlikely since most Filipinos eat five or more meals a day.

Breakfast is often rice and fish or sometimes fried rice and a spicy, local sausage, called *longaniza*, washed down with glasses of ginger tea. Following the Spanish tradition, chocolate is preferred for breakfast by people who can afford it. The beverage is a mixture of chocolate, milk, sugar, and egg white, stirred over low heat. Coffee is also popular among the wealthy for breakfast, as is a glutinous rice dish of an oatmeal-like consistency, flavored with chocolate, and generally eaten with smoked fish. Other delicacies are Chinese ham, sausages, fried or salted eggs, sweet rice cakes garnished with grated coconut; *ensaimada*, a baked roll from dough similar to brioche, topped with grated cheese; and ripe mangoes with cubes of sticky rice. Mid-morning brings more *ensaimada* and hot chocolate, or perhaps a dish of fried noodles. Although quick and easy sandwiches, introduced by the Americans, increasingly stave lunchtime pangs, and rice and soup are mainstays in the middle of the day, lunch cooked in the home is seldom less than a meat dish, such as *caldereta*—a goat stew, grilled fish or shrimp, soup, a cooked vegetable salad, fresh fruit, and a rich dessert. Everything is served at the same time.

Merienda, the famous Philippine meal resembling English high tea, can be anything except steamed rice. Rice constitutes a complete meal and *merienda* is not considered as such, despite the wealth of savory fritters, *lumpia*—spring rolls, noodle dishes, shrimp-filled pancakes, pies, and cakes. Hot chocolate or refreshing *kalamansi* juice is normally the order of the day with *merienda*. Tea is not usually the beverage of choice, except to soothe the throat or the digestion.

For dinner, which is anticipated with enthusiasm, Filipinos will often go to a simple *turo turo* restaurant. The name means point point, and that is exactly how foods are selected, by pointing out a dish from the assortment displayed in the front of the restaurant. If a more elegant restaurant is chosen, dinner could be a savory shellfish soup, an *adobo*—braised pork or chicken with spices, a noodle dish, perhaps an eggplant salad, and, of course, pickles, relishes, and condiments. This may be followed by fruit and one of the exacting desserts which occupy Filipina cooks, such as *gulaman*, a soft melange of pineapple and coconut; *bibingka*, a moist cake made from rice flour and sprinkled with cheese and served with grated coconut; or a thoroughly American slice of lemon meringue pie, or a pie made from guapple (a cross between a guava and an apple).

For many Filipinos, dessert is the highlight of the meal. Often complicated and time-consuming to prepare, a cook's reputation can rest on her skill with confectionery and desserts. Sautés and stir-fries are child's play by comparison. A dessert in a glass, eaten with a spoon, is *halo halo*—although it can be served as a sweet refreshment at any time of day. Reminiscent of Malaysia's ice *kacang*, *halo halo* (the name is Tagalog for mix mix) is the same wild combination of textures and tastes—red beans, corn, shredded coconut, sugar palm seeds, cubes of colored gelatin, and evaporated milk served over crushed ice—but incorporates more kinds of diced fruits and sometimes in addition a generous scoop of coconut or yam ice cream. A more subtle and delicate dessert is made by beating together the soft gelatinous flesh of a very young coconut with its liquid, and sweetening the mixture with sugar before freezing it. Candies and cakes, especially *bibingka*, are eaten as snacks during the day. Filipinos have a taste for sweet cakes garnished with something savory, such as cheese. Unique to the Philippines is a locally made cheese. Made from water buffalo milk, it is aromatic, salty, and lightly pungent. Since cheese is almost unknown in Asian countries, this one almost certainly came into being when the Spanish brought the art of cheese-making with them. Nowadays cheeses from Australia are sold in all supermarkets and other stores.

Spanish Influence in Filipino Culture

But it is Spain that has had by far the greatest influence on the cuisine. When the Spanish first came to Manila, there was already a sizable Chinese colony. Manila was a busy center for trade and commerce since long before the Spanish occupied it in the 1500s, and began building Intramuros, their famed medieval walled city. Inside it boasted a palace for the governor-general, another for the bishop, government offices, schools, a university, a hospital, churches, convents, monasteries, and barracks for soldiers, in case of an emergency. Only Spanish, and people of Spanish descent, were allowed to live in the elegant houses in the enclosed city. Drawbridges over the moat encircling the walls were drawn up at night, barricading the seven heavy gates for added security. Manila is an old colonial town and also a thriving cosmopolitan city with first-class hotels and towering office blocks. Ultramodern shopping centers and elegant boutiques display excellent handwoven fabrics, delicately embroidered blouses, terra-cotta, porcelain, lustrous pearls, and well-made native crafts. Over eight million Filipinos live in Metro Manila. Many fine restaurants serve elegant international dishes from Spain, China, Japan, France, Germany, India, and America. Others specialize in native dishes. Pizza parlors do a very lively business. American restaurants are renowned for their steaks, which are flown in from Australia. Colorful food market aisles display huge piles of fresh fruits and vegetables. Chickens, ducks, and various kinds of meat hang from hooks. Vendors selling sweet and savory snacks, local dishes and drinks, manage to turn out an astonishing array of enticing tidbits. Among these are corn *maya*, a confection made with glutinous rice flour, coconut milk, palm sugar, and corn kernels, embellished with grated coconut; *bokayo* is another coconut treat, this time in the form of fritters; sweet cooking bananas, deep-fried and dipped in syrup; fried sweet potato chunks; crisp shrimp with a savory dipping sauce; *lumpia*; and platters of chicken, fish, and mung beans.

Most towns in the Philippines are built around a central plaza, in the Spanish style, flanked by the town hall and the Catholic church. On market days the town center is thronged with people. Manila, Iloilo, Cebu—the oldest city in the Philippines—and several other towns were planned by the Spanish. Roads leading from the central plazas connect the outlying *barangays*, or barrios as they are still called, with the market towns. *Barangay* is the Pilopino word for village. Pilopino was adopted as the national language in 1937 and its use is increasing. Based on tagalog, a language which has no dialects and is widely understood, Pilopino is an elegant language. Many books have been published in tagalog. Nevertheless, English is commonly spoken, making the Philippines the third largest English-speaking nation in the world.

Filipino taste in food is so close to European palates that it is never a problem for Westerners to find dishes in the Philippine repertoire that are agreeable and delicious, though it might be wise for people with delicate digestions to avoid such dishes as *dinguan*, a strongly flavored stew of blood and beef entrails; and *balut*, a hard-boiled duck egg containing a partly developed embryo—a great delicacy among the Filipinos. Dishes of foreign origin have long since simmered to the top of the ethnic mix and are now considered Filipino. *Adobo* is one example. Others are *paksiw*, a dish of fish or meat cooked in vinegar with ginger, garlic, and salt; *kari kari*, oxtail and beef stew thickened with roasted ground rice and peanuts, sometimes tinted red with annatto seeds; *pesa*, boiled fish with lots of fresh ginger and black pepper; *adobong sugpo*, a tangy yet delicate shrimp dish; *ukoy*, golden, crisp shrimp fritters; chicken *binakol*, a chicken dish sauced with ginger, garlic, soft young coconut meat, and *patis* (fish sauce) packed into a bamboo tube and steamed. Milkfish is readily obtainable and much loved by the Filipinos, although, like shad, it requires expert boning. One delicious dish is prepared by stuffing the boned fish with ground pork, red bell peppers, and tomatoes, seasoned with *kalamansi* and soy sauce. *Suman* is a sweet dessert that can be made from glutinous rice, *saba* bananas, or cassava. It is generally cooked in a bamboo tube and served with palm sugar and freshly grated coconut. This is one of the Filipinos' favorite desserts.

Ubiquitous in the cooking of the Philippines are *bagoong balayan*, a pungent, thick sauce of fermented small fish, *bagoong alamang*, a chunkier, pink paste of salted, tiny shrimps, and *patis*, a clear amber-colored fish sauce. Variations of these fish-based sauces, most of them somewhat stronger in flavor than the Philippine versions, are used in every Southeast Asian country. Without them the marvelous cuisines of this region would be unrecognizable.

Mixing different types of food together is common throughout Filipino cuisine. Pork, chicken, fish, shellfish, and vegetables may be, and frequently are, mixed in one dish, usually with a base of garlic sautéd in olive oil. No single taste predominates: the blend is the flavor. *Adobo*, for instance, combines all the Filipinos' favorite tastes and techniques: vinegar, peppercorns, garlic, and bay leaves marinate a mixture of pork, chicken, and perhaps shellfish. The meat and fish are cooked in the marinade with added soy sauce, then fried a deep brown in lard, and further simmered with broth, sour vegetables and fruits until the sauce reaches the desired consistency. Coconut milk and *bagoong* (shrimp paste) are also acceptable additions to *adobo*, depending on the whim of the cook. As *adobo* keeps very well and improves with time, cooks usually prepare it at least a day in advance. *Sinigang*, an extremely sour soup, served piping hot, is made with a flavorful broth of meat and chicken or fish and shellfish, and cooked with tomatoes, sour fruits, and sour vegetables. Traditionally it is brought to the table in an earthenware dish, called a *palayok*.

Fiesta Specialties

Spanish dishes are always served at fiestas and at other important occasions. Fiestas dot the Philippine religious calendar, many of them celebrating the same events as the original pagan festivals, such as harvest thanksgiving. With the advent of Catholicism, Christian saints took the place of pagan gods. Since each village has its own patron saint, and each saint an annual festival, there is always a religious celebration going on somewhere. Major Catholic festivals are Easter and Christmas. The Chinese and Muslims have their own religious fiestas, and everybody celebrates New Year—although not always at the same time. On top of all this activity, personal fiestas can be held for weddings, christenings, and any other significant family occasion.

All fiestas have in common an abundance of food and drink. For poorer people, fiestas are often the only time they are able to eat meat. Dishes are elaborate and expensive. Vegetables are considered too pedestrian for special occasions, so most dishes weighing down the table are meat dishes, such as *caldereta, morcon, kari kari*, and boned chicken stuffed with ground meats and sausage. The favorite centerpiece is *lechon*, a whole roast suckling pig, stuffed with rice and tamarind leaves, and spit-roasted over burning coals. The pig's liver is made into a rich sauce, spiced with pepper, garlic, and onions. Before the carver sets to work, the assembled guests pinch off the crisp skin with their fingertips, beginning at the ears and ending at the tail. The meal ends with the most luscious of seasonal fruits and traditional candies. *Yema* is a delicious confection of egg yokes and sugar. Pastillas de leche, in an assortment of colors and fruit flavors, is based on water buffalo milk. The finished candy is rolled in white sugar and wrapped in rice paper. Many fruits lend themselves to candy making. Cooked down to form a stiff paste, the candy is then molded into the shape of the original fruit.

Fiestas start with High Mass, followed by street processions, gaudy floats on the waterways, marching bands, sporting events, and, at night, a fireworks display against the night sky. Some Philippine fiestas, in particular the Ati-Atihan in Kalibo, the Dinagyang in Iloilo, and the Sinulog in Cebu, have escalated into huge mardi-gras affairs, losing some of their original flavor.

Regional food differences are found between the islands. The Ilocanos, for example, prefer vegetables to meat and eat great quantities of them. One of their favorite dishes is bitter melon, okra, green beans, and eggplants seasoned with shrimp paste. They make interesting dishes with cabbages, radishes, squash, and wild local leaves, almost always flavoring the melange with one of the fish-based fermented sauces.

Muslim from Mindanao are famed for their *tinola*, a fish soup seasoned with onions and tomatoes. Another Muslim dish, *utak-utak*, is a patty of flaked fish, lightly mixed with beaten egg and spices, before frying. On Cebu, in the Visayas, corn is the staple food of at least a fifth of the people. In areas where it rains frequently, as many as four crops of corn are grown each year. On Luzon rice is the staple. Banaue, on Luzon, is the site of the majestic Rice Terraces which were carved from the mountains 3,000 years ago, using simple hand tools. A natural irrigation system flows down from the top.

Rice and fish are the staple foods of the Philippines. Rice is eaten three times a day, at breakfast, lunch, and dinner. It is also made into noodles, and ground into rice flour for the many esteemed desserts, cakes, and pancakes. Fish is eaten every day, especially in villages where people are too poor to buy meat. Pork, however, is more prevalent, as people often keep pigs which are able to root around for their food. The seas lapping the shores of the Philippines provide enough fish to nourish almost all the people living on the islands. Species of fish number 2,400, including at least five types of sea turtles providing protein-rich eggs—considered a great delicacy. Snapper, mackerel, sea bass, tuna, grouper, cuttlefish, shellfish, and dozens of other different sea creatures find their way into Asian cooking pots. Since refrigeration is not nationally available, drying, salting, and especially fermenting are techniques routinely used to preserve the catch. Much of the fish is taken directly from the fishermen to the market. Filipinos expect their fish to be fresh enough to leap from the market scales. *Kilawin*, a dish of raw fish or shellfish, lightly marinated in lime juice, is their favorite method of preparation. Failing that, they like it grilled over coals.

Alcohol is a part of life in the Philippines, excepting Muslims. Bars are numerous, and gin, rum, and whiskey are reasonably priced when compared to other Asian countries. San Miguel is the favorite beer. Vineyards in the Visayas produce wine and various kinds of local toddies. *Tuba* is made from the sap of the coconut palm, and *lampanog*, a more potent brew, is distilled from the same source. *Tapuy* is a wine made from rice, and *basi* is wine made from sugarcane. Soft drinks and iced fruit juices are also sold everywhere. Coffee houses are increasing. Ginger tea and ginger coffee are sometimes made for breakfast.

Cooking Philippine food in an American kitchen is easy, as most Filipinas have much the same utensils as we have, and prefer to use western saucepans, skillets, and baking dishes. A Philippine wok, called a *carajay*, is similar to any wok you would find in the West. Traditional earthenware pots, lined with banana leaves to prevent sticking, are still used to cook rice in some outlying villages. But in the cities, heavy-bottomed saucepans are taking the place of earthenware. Some people believe food tastes better when eaten with the fingers, and there are one or two restaurants that cater to this preference.

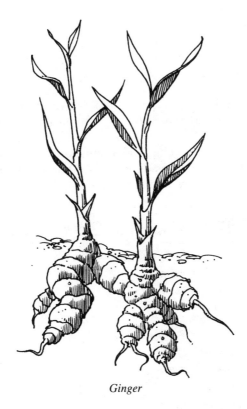

Ginger

However, tableware has also been westernized in the cities, and dinner plates, knives, forks, and spoons are in regular use.

Recipes from the Philippines

Fish Fillets with Black Bean and Tomato Sauce

¼	C.	light sesame oil
12	oz.	thick, white fish fillets
2		shallots, sliced
2	t.	ginger, finely shredded
2		garlic cloves, minced
3	T.	homemade tomato sauce
4	t.	fermented black beans, rinsed and chopped

1 T.	Japanese rice vinegar
½ C.	water
1–2 t.	sugar
½ t.	salt

Cut fillet into one-inch pieces. Heat oil and sauté the fish until golden. Remove with slotted spoon to paper towels and keep warm. Stir the shallots, ginger, and garlic into the oil and stir-fry until the onion softens. Add the remaining ingredients, and simmer for 3 minutes. Carefully return the pieces of fish to the hot sauce, ladle sauce over fish to coat completely, and simmer for 2 minutes more.   *Serves 2*

Golden Bean Curd and Bean Sprout Salad

2 C.	bean sprouts, trimmed
¼ C.	peanut or sesame oil
1 C.	firm bean curd, sliced
2	shallots, sliced
2 T.	shrimp sauce or anchovy paste
1 t.	red pepper flakes
	juice of one lime
2 T.	minced cilantro

Blanch bean sprouts for 2 minutes in boiling water. Drain and set aside. Heat 2 tablespoonsful of oil in wok and fry bean curd until brown. Remove with a slotted spoon to paper towels to drain. Fry shallots until golden in same oil, drain on paper towels.

Place bean sprouts and bean curd in a medium-sized salad bowl. Whisk together remaining oil, shrimp sauce or anchovy paste, red pepper flakes, and lime juice and pour over salad, tossing lightly. Garnish with shallots and minced cilantro.   *Serves 4*

Lightly Spiced Shrimp

2	T.	peanut oil
3–4		garlic cloves, minced
12	oz.	fresh shrimp, shelled and deveined
¼	C.	homemade dense tomato sauce OR 1 medium-sized ripe tomato, peeled, seeded, and diced
2	t.	hot chili purée
3	T.	Chinese rice wine
1	T.	fresh lemon juice
		pinch of sugar
4	oz.	fresh snow peas, trimmed
1	T.	minced cilantro for garnish

Heat oil in wok over medium-high heat, add garlic, and brown lightly.
Add shrimp, turn heat to high, and stir-fry for 1 minute. Stir in tomato
sauce or diced tomato, chili purée, rice wine, lemon juice, and sugar.
Stir for 30 seconds. Add snow peas and stir for 30 seconds more.
Remove to warmed serving dish, garnish with cilantro, and serve imme-
diately with rice. *Serves 2–3*

Chicken Pochero

3	lb.	cut-up chicken
1		chorizo sausage
1	T.	black peppercorns
1	t.	salt
1		potato, peeled and cut in chunks
1	medium	sweet potato, peeled and cut in chunks

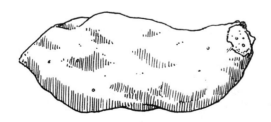

Sweet potato

⅓ lb.   green beans, trimmed
½ small   head of cabbage, shredded
2   plantains
2 T.   corn oil
2   garlic cloves, minced
1 small   onion, minced
6 T.   tomato paste
1 C.   tomato, seeded and diced
⅔ C.   cooking liquid
½ C.   canned chick peas

Place chicken in a heavy-bottomed, lidded pan and cover with water. Add chorizo, peppercorns, and salt, cover, and simmer for 25 minutes. Reserving cooking liquid, drain the chicken and chorizo, and keep them warm. Simmer green beans in the cooking liquid for 8 minutes. Remove with a slotted spoon and set aside. Add the potato and sweet potato to the cooking liquid and simmer, partially covered, until soft. Add the cabbage to the pot, bring to the boil, simmer 1 minute, and remove from heat. The liquid will have simmered down to a thick sauce. Set aside.

Meanwhile, cook the plantain separately for 5–10 minutes, peel and set aside with the chicken. Cut chorizo into hearty slices. Heat oil in a skillet, and sauté the garlic and onion until the onion begins to soften. Add and sauté the chorizo until browned. Add the tomato paste, diced tomato, cooking liquid, and chick peas, and simmer for 5 minutes. Season with ground black pepper and salt, if necessary. Serve the chicken napped with the tomato sauce and surrounded by vegetables, chorizo, and sauce.

Serves 6

Pork Adobo

4   jalapeno peppers, grilled
3   hot fleshy peppers, such as poblano, grilled
1½ C.   orange juice
½ medium   onion, sliced
1   head of garlic cloves, peeled
⅓ C.   cider vinegar
1 t.   cumin seeds
1 t.   coriander seeds
½   cinnamon stick

2 T.	soy sauce
1 t.	salt
3½ lb.	loin of pork
2 T.	lard or shortening

Remove seeds and most of the skin from the peppers. Warm orange juice, and purée with the peppers, onion, and garlic in a food processor. Stir in vinegar. Use a spice grinder or a mortar and pestle to grind the cumin, coriander, and cinnamon. Add spices and salt to purée. Place meat in a nonreactive lidded dish. Pour mixture over meat, cover, and refrigerate for at least 6 hours or overnight. Remove dish from refrigerator an hour before starting to cook meat. Preheat oven to 350°F. Scrape sauce from meat back into the dish. Slather the loin with lard or shortening. Roast for about 30 minutes per pound, basting often with the sauce. The internal temperature of the meat should reach 165°. Remove meat from oven and sear in a large skillet for a minute or two each side to brown. Set on a warmed serving dish. Degrease sauce in roasting pan, boil, briefly, with any leftover marinade, and serve with the sliced loin. The sauce will be heavy and spicy—use as you would horseradish. *Serves 6*

Green Beans and Mushrooms with Sesame Seeds

1 lb.	fresh green beans, sliced thinly into two in lengths
3 T.	peanut oil

½ lb.   button mushrooms, halved
1 T.   dark sesame oil
2 T.   soy sauce
         freshly ground black pepper
2 T.   sesame seeds, toasted

Cook beans in boiling salted water for 3 minutes. Drain. Heat 2 table-spoons of peanut oil in a wok, and stir-fry the mushrooms for 2 or 3 minutes. Add the well-drained beans and stir-fry for 1 minute. Sprinkle vegetables with the dark sesame oil, pour in the soy sauce, and season with black pepper. Simmer, covered, for 3 or 4 minutes longer. Serve sprinkled with sesame seeds.   *Serves 2–3*

Shrimp Fritters

12 oz.   small shrimp, shelled, deveined
1   egg
½ C.   water
1 t.   fish sauce
¾ C.   flour
½ t.   salt
           freshly ground black pepper, to taste
2 small   shallots, finely sliced
½ small   red chili, seeded and finely minced
⅓ C.   peanut or corn oil for frying

Lightly process half of the shrimp in a food processor, or pound with a mortar and pestle. Cut the remaining shrimp in half lengthwise. Beat the egg with the water and fish sauce. Place the flour in a mixing bowl, and gradually beat in the egg water mixture. Season with salt and pepper and thoroughly stir in the processed shrimp paste. If the mixture is very thick, add more water a little at a time. The batter should have the consistency of thick yogurt. Fold in the remaining sliced shrimp, the shallots, and the minced chili. Heat the oil in a large skillet or an electric fry pan, and pour in about 2 tablespoons of batter at a time. Fry until golden, turn and fry the other side. Do not crowd pan. Remove to paper towels to drain. Serve as a side dish.

Bibingka—Cake with Cheese and Grated Coconut

3		eggs
1	t.	vanilla extract (optional)
2	C.	flour
2	t.	baking powder
1	t.	salt
1¼	C.	coconut milk
¾	C.	sugar
¼	C.	melted butter
3	oz.	goat cheese, crumbled
2	t.	sugar for garnish
⅓	C.	toasted grated coconut for garnish

Preheat oven to 375°F. Grease a 9-inch cake pan. In a small bowl, beat eggs and add vanilla extract if using. Sift together flour, baking powder, and salt. Pour coconut milk into a large mixing bowl, add sugar, and stir to dissolve. Beat eggs into coconut milk mixture. With a wooden spoon, fold in flour. Pour into cake pan and bake for 15 minutes. Quickly drizzle half of melted butter quickly on cake. Bake 15 minutes. Repeat with the remaining butter. Bake for 5 minutes more or until a cake tester comes out clean. Remove to cake rack; after 5 minutes, sprinkle goat cheese on cake, followed by sugar. Allow cake to cool for another 10 minutes. Gently spread goat cheese in center of cake in a rough circle and sprinkle with toasted, grated coconut.   Serves 8–12

GLOSSARY

A*chuete* or annatto seeds give a red color and a mild peppery flavor to Filipino foods, such as *ukoy*—shrimp and potato cakes. They were introduced to the Philippines by the Spaniards. If they are not available, it is possible to substitute a small amount of paprika.

B*agoong*—*see shrimp paste*

B*anana flowers* These heavy, large, dark buds are available canned in Asian markets and are usually imported from the Philippines. Drain and rinse well before using.

B*anana leaf* Banana leaves are used to wrap foods before steaming or grilling. Secure the package with a bamboo skewer or by tying it with kitchen string. The banana leaf will add its own unique, delicate flavor to the food. Banana leaves, obtainable in Asian markets, need to be soaked in hot water until they are pliable, and cleaned with a dampened cloth before using.

B*ean curd sheets* Bean curd sheets are used to wrap foods. Soak them in warm water until they become pliable—usually about 5 minutes. They are very fragile, and tear easily. Holes can be patched by dampening the edges of the damaged areas and layering with another piece of bean curd sheet.

B*ean curd, fresh, dried, and fermented* **(tempe)** Fresh bean curds, packed in water, are widely available in supermarkets and Asian markets. Both soft and firm bean curds are best used as soon as possible. If necessary they can be kept refrigerated up to a week, if the water surrounding the curd is changed daily. Firm bean curd is more suitable than soft bean curd for slicing, or cubing for stir-frying. Drain off the liquid before bean curd for slicing, or cubing for stir-frying. Drain off the liquid before using. Dried bean curd can be reconstituted in water or dropped into soupy dishes to reconstitute in the sauce. Tempe is fermented bean curd. They are all high in protein and inexpensive.

Bean sauces, black and yellow Readily obtainable in Asian markets, these sauces are made from black or yellow preserved beans. Their tastes are almost identical and the choice between them depends solely on the color of the food being prepared.

Belacan—*see dried shrimp paste*

Besan, chick pea flour Used to thicken sauces, chick pea flour is made from roasted ground chick peas. Its distinctive taste has no substitute, but it is usually obtainable in Asian markets.

Candlenuts Candlenuts are ground into curry pastes and other Southeast Asian sauces as a thickener. The nut is a little larger in size than a chick pea and very hard. The oil content of a candlenut is so high, it can be set alight and used as a candle—hence the name. Macadamia nuts, used at a ratio of one and a half macadamia nuts to one candlenut, are a good substitute.

Cardamom seeds The tiny black seeds within the husk of a cardamom seed have a sweet, warm flavor that is ground into curry pastes, and Indian rice dishes such as *biryani* and *pilau*. One of the most expensive spices in the world, cardamom flavors Arab coffee and many Mediterranean dishes. In Europe cardamom is used in desserts and baked goods, especially those using nuts and dried fruits.

Cellophane noodles Cellophane noodles are thin, transparent noodles made from mung bean starch. Frequently added to soups, they can be soaked in warm water, or boiled for a few seconds, before adding to a finished dish.

Chili peppers Chili peppers grow profusely and cross-pollinate to such an extent that it is sometimes impossible to know the taste of each variety without sampling a small piece of the flesh—without the seeds or ribs. A general rule is that the smaller the pepper, the hotter it is. Usually the hottest chilies, such as the tiny "bird" chili, are found only in Asian markets. Wear rubber gloves when handling hot chili peppers, and wash gloves, hands, and knives when finished, as the hot oils can be very painful around sensitive areas, particularly the eyes.

Chili sauce Obtainable in jars in supermarkets and Asian markets, this hot, spicy red sauce can be used in any dish where chili peppers are called for.

Chili peppers

Chinese dried mushrooms Dried mushrooms have an intense flavor. The large shiitake mushrooms need to be soaked for about 30 minutes and thoroughly washed to remove any impurities. Discard the tough stems. Smaller mushrooms are soaked for less time, or can be added to a dish to reconstitute in the sauce during cooking. Microwave ovens shorten the soaking time considerably.

Coconut cream and milk Coconut cream is made by squeezing the liquid from grated, fresh coconut. Coconut milk is the second squeezing, after some water has been added. Both are readily obtainable in cans in Asian markets. It is possible to freeze leftover coconut milk; if frozen, do not thaw, but add it directly to the cooking pot.

Coriander (cilantro, Chinese parsley) Fresh leaves from the coriander plant, also called cilantro or Chinese parsley, garnish many Southeast Asian foods. The taste is somewhat bitter and pungent and it is a good foil for creamy coconut-enriched foods. Coriander seed adds a warm, citrus flavor to dishes using garlic and chili. It is also good with meats and in sausage mixtures. Since its taste is not overpowering, it may be used generously. The taste of the seeds is completely unlike the taste of the leaves. Coriander root is pounded and mixed with other ingredients for Southeast Asian marinades.

Cumin Cumin has a nutty, aromatic taste, and is used frequently in Asian and Mediterranean foods. The light tan seed is shaped like a caraway seed. Cumin is a member of the parsley family of plants. Store in a cool, dark place and replace after six months.

Curry pastes: **Red curry, Green curry, Yellow curry** Red, green, and yellow prepared curry pastes are obtainable in Asian markets. The red color is from paprika and red chilies, the green from green chilies, and the yellow from turmeric and yellow or orange chilies. They are all very hot. Usually made in Thailand, they are popular throughout Southeast Asia as they are reliable and give predictable results.

Fennel seeds Ground fennel seeds are added to curries. The seed has a subtle aniseed taste that pairs well with fish. Fennel is one of the ingredients in the five spice powder used ubiquitously in Chinese food wherever it is found.

Fenugreek Fenugreek seeds are an essential ingredient in curry powders and pastes. They have a pungent taste and a distinctive aroma. They should be lightly roasted before grinding, as they turn bitter when overcooked. Fenugreek is used in small quantities in Indian vegetable dishes.

Fish sauce Fish sauce is made by packing small fish with salt in a barrel and leaving them to ferment. The best quality sauce is from the first draining from the barrel. This is an amber-colored, clear liquid with a good aroma, especially if it has been made only with anchovies. Lesser grades of fish sauce are made by adding water after the first draining. Fish sauce is used in almost every savory dish in Southeast Asia, and in all dipping sauce recipes.

Five spice powder A combination of ground cloves, fennel, cinnamon, star anise, and Szechuan peppercorns, five spice powder is used in practically all Chinese savory dishes.

Galangal Galangal root is similar to gingerroot, but with a pinkish translucent skin. It is also thicker and heavier in size than ginger.

Gingerroot Ginger's pronounced, slightly hot, aromatic flavor is blended into curry pastes and powders and is used frequently in sauces in Southeast Asian cooking. It is always used fresh, and can be grated, shredded, or sliced. Ginger tea and ginger coffee are popular in the Philippines, Indonesia, and Malaysia.

Glutinous rice Glutinous or sticky rice is short-grained, almost round in shape, and when steamed it clumps together unlike long-grained rice. Glutinous rice is served at all meals in Laos. Most other Southeast Asian countries keep sticky rice for making desserts and snacks. Glutinous rice can be grilled and ground to make a flour popular in Laos.

Holy basil Holy basil has a stronger flavor than regular sweet basil. Its leaf and flower buds have a definite purple cast. When substituting sweet basil for Holy basil, use double the quantity called for in the recipe.

Gingerroot

Kaffir lime Kaffir lime is larger, and the skin more pitted and lumpy, than the skin of regular limes. The tart juice is used in dishes both savory and sweet, and the zest is grated into curry pastes. Kaffir lime leaves, small, round, and glossy, are thinly slivered and added to soups, curries, and many other savory dishes. Kaffir lime leaves are obtainable at Asian markets. Regular lime zest and juice can be substituted for Kaffir lime.

Kecap manis This sauce is a sweet version of soy sauce that also includes garlic, ginger, and star anise. It is used extensively in Indonesia, and is available in Asian markets in jars. A substitute is to mix dark soy sauce with brown sugar.

Laos This spice is a form of ginger that is used in its powdered form. It is very mildly flavored and may be used generously.

Lemongrass This dry bulbous grass grows in Asia, Australia, and in southern states in America. The outer leaves are stripped away and the inner bulb, and four or five inches of the pliable inner stalk, are sliced or pounded for use in Asian dishes. It imparts a lemony flavor and fragrance to foods. Lemongrass can be frozen successfully and is also

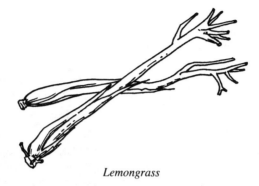

Lemongrass

available in dried form. It is obtainable in some supermarkets and in Asian markets.

Nam pla (Thailand)—*see fish sauce*

Ngan pye pa (Myanmar)—*see shrimp paste*

Ngapi (Myanmar)—*see fish sauce*

Nuoc mam (Vietnam)—*see fish sauce*

Padek (Laos) Made from chunky fermented fish and brine. Both the brine and the fish chunks may be used separately.

Palm sugar Palm sugar, also called jaggery, is made from the sap of the coconut palm. The sap, boiled until it crystallizes, is usually sold in cakes. Dark brown sugar can be substituted.

Pandan leaves Pandan leaves from the screwpine tree, pounded and boiled, are used to flavor desserts in Indonesia, Malaysia, and Singapore, much as we add vanilla essence. They may also be used as an additional flavoring in curries and rice dishes.

Patis (Philippines)—*see fish sauce*

Peanuts Unsalted, raw peanuts are roasted, chopped, and used as a garnish with savory and sweet dishes in Southeast Asia. They may also be pounded with other ingredients to thicken a spice paste. *Satays* in Southeast Asia are invariably accompanied by a peanut sauce, spiked with chilies.

Petis (Indonesia and Malaysia)—*see shrimp paste*

Pickled cabbage Pickled cabbage is a favorite relish served to complement savory dishes in Southeast Asia. It is obtainable canned in Asian markets.

Preserved radish Grated preserved radish is added to savory foods in Southeast Asia both for its sharp flavor and for texture. It should be used sparingly. It is obtainable in Asian markets.

Rice cakes Rice cakes are usually molded from cooked sticky rice. Left to air-dry, they are then either crisply fried or steamed, and served as a snack or to accompany other dishes at meals.

Rice flour Rice flour is as finely ground as cornstarch, which can be substituted for rice flour. It may be used to thicken sauces. Many dessert recipes use rice flour, or a mixture of rice flour and wheat flour. Rice stick noodles and rice vermicelli, both sold dried in supermarkets and Asian markets, are made with rice flour.

Rice wrappers These thin, almost translucent wrappers are rolled around delectable fillings to make spring rolls, or *lumpia*, as they are called in the Philippines. Obtainable in Asian markets, they will need to be either dipped for a second in boiling water or brushed with beaten egg white to make them pliable enough to roll.

Sago Sago is the dried pith of the sago palm which, when ground, yields a granular flour. The sago palm grows in India and Malaysia. Bread and desserts can be made from sago. If sago is not accessible, cream of wheat makes a good substitute.

Saki Saki, Japanese rice wine, is a national favorite in its country of origin, where it is usually served warm. Used to add a distinctive flavor to many oriental dishes, it can replace sherry in any recipe.

Shrimp paste Shrimp paste is obtainable in Asian markets in jars and plastic boxes. Its odor is powerful. It is not necessary to refrigerate it, but it is best kept in an airtight container. Shrimp paste is very salty and should be used sparingly. It also needs to be cooked. When adding it to the cooking pot, crush the paste against the side of the pot with a wooden spoon, mix well with other ingredients, and cook for at least 5 minutes. If it is to be added to an uncooked dipping sauce or salad dressing, fold the shrimp sauce in aluminum foil and grill for 5 minutes on each side. Crumble the cooked shrimp paste into the sauce and blend well.

Shrimp, dried Dried shrimp, whole or powdered, are obtainable in Asian markets. These two products are used almost daily in sauces, salads, soups, and noodle dishes for flavor and for texture. Keep them in an airtight container.

Soybeans, salted Obtainable in Asian markets in jars or cans, these fermented black beans need to be briefly soaked and rinsed to remove the salt. Packed with flavor, they are wonderful used in savory sauces accompanied by lots of garlic.

Soy sauce Widely available in supermarkets and Asian markets, soy sauce adds a salty taste to many Asian dishes. It will keep indefinitely without

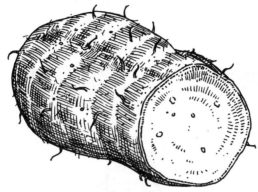

Taro root

refrigeration. Japanese soy sauce has a flavor that is different enough from Chinese soy sauce that they are not interchangeable.

Star anise Star anise is one of the ingredients in five spice powder. Star anise is frequently used in Chinese and Southeast Asian cooking. It is a dark brown, star-shaped, dried spice consisting of eight pods. Star anise adds a licorice taste to foods, and it is often added to a dish whole and removed just before serving.

Tamarind Tamarind is in frequent use in Southeast Asian cooking where it is prized for its sharp, tart flavor. The long, beanlike pods of the tamarind tree have a large seed, encased in a dark brown fruity pulp. The pulp and seeds are obtainable in jars or in blocks in Asian markets, and will need to be soaked in warm water for 10 minutes, before straining out the seeds. Both the pulp and the young leaves of the tamarind are used in Asian cooking. If tamarind is not accessible, substitute twice the amount of tamarind called for in the recipe with lemon juice.

Taro root Taro root is a starchy tuber that is steamed until soft, puréed, and mixed with sweet ingredients, such as coconut cream and sugar, to make desserts.

Trassi—*see shrimp paste*

Turmeric root Turmeric root is obtainable fresh and ground in Southeast Asia. It adds a lovely orange color to foods, and to curry powder. Turmeric is a member of the ginger family of rhizomes. It has a warm, spicy taste and a pleasant aroma. It should not be used in place of saffron—the delicate dried stamen of the purple crocus—as they have widely different tastes.

BIBLIOGRAPHY

Thailand

Hans Hofer, revised by Steve Van Beek, *Thailand* APA *Insight Guides*. APA PUBLICATIONS (HK) LTD., 1991.
Thailand Seven Days in the Kingdom. Times Editions, 1987.
Vatcharin Bhumichitr, *A Taste of Thailand*. Atheneum, New York, NY, 1988.
Charlie Amatyakul, ed. John Mitchell, *A Taste of Thailand*. Asia Books, Bangkok, Thailand, 1982.

Myanmar (Burma)

Wilhelm Klein, *Burma* APA *Insight Guides*. APA PUBLICATIONS (HK) LTD., 1989.
V. C. Scott O'Connor, *Mandalay and Other Cities of the Past in Burma*. London: Hutchinson & Co. Paternoster Row, 1907. (White Lotus Co., Ltd.)
John Lowry, *Burmese Art—The Victoria and Albert Museum*. H.M.S. Printing Office: Crown Copyright, 1974.
Mi Mi Khaing, *The World of Burmese Women*. Singapore: Time Books International, 1984.
R. Talbot Kelly, *BURMA—Painted and Described*. London: Adam and Charles Black, 1905.
Henry Yule, *Narrative of the Mission to the Court of Ava in 1855*. Oxford University Press, Oxford, England, 1968.
L. Bharadwaya, *History of Burma Made Easy*. 1959.

Khin Myo Chit, A *Wonderland of Burmese Legends*. The Tamarind Press, Bangkok, Thailand, 1984.

Shway Yoe, *The Burman His Life and Notions*. London: Macmillan & Co., 1927. (First ed. 1882, second ed. 1896, third ed. 1910, Reprinted 1927.)

Mi Mi Khaing, *Cook and Entertain the Burmese Way*. Daw Ma Ma Kin, Student Press, Raropou, Burma, 1975.

Laos

Ralph Zickgraf, *Laos Places and Peoples of the World*. Chelsea House Publishers, a division of Main Line Book Co., 1991.

Alan Davidson, *Fish and Fish Dishes of Laos*, with drawings by Elian Prasith Souvannavong, Thao Soun, and Thao Singha. Imprimerie Nationale Vientiane, 1975.

Phia Sing, *Traditional ·Recipes of Laos*. Prospect Books, Chelsea, London, UK,1981.

Renée de Berval, *Kingdom of Laos—France-Asie, Saigon, Vietnam*. 1959.

Vietnam

Daniel Robinson and Joe Cummings, *Vietnam, Laos and Cambodia—Lonely Planet Travel Survival Kit*. Lonely Planet, Berkeley, CA, 1991.

Bach Ngo and Gloria Zimmerman, *The Classic Cuisine of Vietnam*. Barron's Educational Series, Inc., 1979, 1986.

Malaysia

Geoffrey Eu, revised by Susan Amy, *Malaysia APA Insight Guides*. APA PUBLICATIONS (HK) LTD., 1990.

Stella Martin and Denis Walls, *In Malaysia*. UK: Bradt Publications, 1986.

Singapore

David Low and Alice Thompson, *Singapore with Excursion to Malaysia—Fodor* 1989.

Singapore Insight Guides. APA PUBLICATIONS (HK) Ltd., 1989.

Cecilia Tan, *Penang Nyonya Cooking*. Singapore: Times Book, International.

Indonesia

Copeland Marks, *The Exotic Kitchens of Indonesia*. New York: M. Evans and Company, 1989.

Charmaine Solomon, *The Complete Asian Cookbook*. Kevin Weldon & Associates Pty Limited 1976. Rutland, Vermont and Tokyo, Japan: Charles E. Tuttle, 1992.

Ruth Law, *Southeast Asia Cookbook*. New York: Donald I. Fine, Inc., 1990.

Jennifer Brennan, *One-Dish Meals of Asia*. Harper Perennial, New York, NY, 1985.

The Philippines

Peter Harper and Evelyn Peplow, *The Philippines Handbook*. Moon Publications, Chico, CA, 1991.

Eleanor Laquian and Irene Sobrevinas, *Filipino Cooking Here and Abroad*. Metro Manila: National Book Store, Publishers, 1977.

RECIPE INDEX

SUBJECT INDEX